Condensation and Condescension in Dreams and History

Essay - From Sigmund Freud to E P Thompson

Anil Pundlik Gokhale

authorHOUSE®

AuthorHouse™ UK Ltd.
500 Avebury Boulevard
Central Milton Keynes, MK9 2BE
www.authorhouse.co.uk
Phone: 08001974150

First published by AuthorHouse 11/17/2008

ISBN: 978-1-4343-3859-4 (sc)

Printed in the United States of America
Bloomington, Indiana

This book is printed on acid-free paper.

Dedicated

To the memory of Paul Ricouer-
the talented exponent of Science and Art of Interpretation

Index

ACKNOWLEDGEMENTS AND CREDITS

This book has been the result of last few years of my work on a subject which has been addressed by a very few Authors. It has been my dream to publish it and I express my gratitude to Author House for agreeing to publish it and extending most valuable assistance in helping me to Edit the Manuscript a few times and providing me appropriate cover page. I am thankful to Timothy Fitch, Gregory Eckart, Liam Brandom and others to guide me through the revisions of the Manuscript.

In early phase the idea of writing on this subject originated in the prolonged discussions I have been having with my friend J. Ulians who has been a prolific reader on updates on psychoanalytic literature and who had been undergoing psychoanalytic treatment for last two decades. Few of the ideas and insights discussed in this book are the result of my interactions and discussions with him and other friends having interest in human sciences.

The subject, 'Dreams & History' relationship was maturing in my mind for more than a decade after witnessing the spontaneous upheaval and subsequent plight of hundreds of textile mill worker activists. Their sufferings from various psychological disorders subsequent to the crushing defeat of the longest ever, textile mill worker strike in Mumbai during 1984-85 has become overwhelming concern for various organizations, Institutes and centers engaged in their rehabilitation activities.

One of the recent inspiring work on History -'Oral History' of The Mill Workers of Mumbai' is an attempt to rescue the history which faces the grave danger of being forgotten'. This novel book hit the book stands (One Hundred years, One Hundred Voices-2004-Author Ms. Meera Adarkar and Meena Menon). Despite being a brave attempt to rescue the vanquished heroes of History the book has limitations of enquiring within the confines of the 'Oral- Spoken' and interpretation of 'un-spoken word' remains beyond its scope.

Depth comprehension will require very sophisticated techniques and methodology and research work of historical analysis of the past and to reach into the remains of 'unspoken', 'unknown' and 'Unconscious'.

In this sense my book is a preparatory one for those interested in History.

These fascinating sophisticated techniques were first formulated with precision by Sigmund Freud and the visual illustrations of these techniques were popularized by 'Freud Museum' London. I am grateful to the Museum and to Michael Molnar (Director- Freud Museum London) and Rita Aspan (Shop and Marketing) for their valuable help in permitting me to down load and use the visual illustrations and images from web site www.freud.org.uk .

I am also thankful to renowned Marxist Historian Carl Schorske who, on my personal request, couriered to me his photograph for publication in this book and I could use the photographs in image captioned as 'Critiques'.

The Design of Book Cover page became possible because of availability of very expressive and appropriate images in Author House approved web site www.shutterstock.com and could represent the core content of the subject of the book.

The book has fired my desire to dream of establishing an History Research Institute in Mumbai dedicated to three founding fathers, of 'psycho history', Karl Marx, Sigmund Freud and E.P. Thompson and hope that it will not remain my 'phantasy!

Lastly I cannot avoid acknowledging the crucial support rendered to me by my wife Vasanti, to whom I will remain indebted. Without her help and encouragement it would not have been possible to steer through the publication of this book.

Preface

In this essay, 'Condensation and condescension in Dreams and history,' as the Title suggest, I have attempted to explore the possible applications of great Freudian discoveries in his discourse on interpretation of dreams for Historical Research methodology. In doing so I have confined myself to enunciate what are those discoveries and how they can be applied to 'past epochs' called history.

Freud's pathological investigations into dream image, the first member of psychological disorders, have led him to understand more comprehensive problems of pathology.

For me Freud's peculiar investigation methodology and his ability to weld new techniques of interpretation, and method of psychoanalytic treatment enabled him to get fabulous and great insights into two important disciplines. They are namely 'psycho-archeology' and 'history'. His ideas as I read them, particularly his great founding works of psychoanalysis, Interpretation of Dreams, which consumed me more and more, to the extent that with obsession I searched further for next few years to look out for application methodology of psychoanalysis to history.

In this process I confronted a few great philosopher-historians, critics and admirers of Freud in his discipline and who have been great commentators and interpreters of Sigmund Freud and psychoanalysis. To my surprise and astonishment one of the greatest historians of our times, E.P. Thompson had already treated history as a process in the manner close to what I was searching for, in his book, "Making of the English Working Class". But it was not so easy to establish what can be the common ground on which they stand is.

I read E.P. Thompson with hunger and discovered that he has used, number of psychoanalytic' techniques as part of his research method in History, without even a single reference to Sigmund Freud and his works! This he did it, probably, without even knowing, under the influence of Erich From, his comrade in 'New Left Review', or to a great extent due to some reasons which compelled him to articulate 'himself'. All his efforts were ***directed to rescue the great mass of working men and women who contributed to making of history and perished without leaving a significant mark on history***. They were the forgotten heroes! What involved for him was 'rewriting or rather re-interpreting' history. The sources which he had to lay hands were not easily available. It involved making every thing 'upside down' and that compelled him to device new techniques of enquiry into what lies 'buried' under the repression of posterity. I also guess that the book involves 'self analysis' of a 'Methodist'.

I rejoiced myself and my findings, my insights and named the new discipline as 'psycho-history'. Again I was at surprise to find that to write 'psycho-history' has been a pursuit of some historians who can be counted on fingers. But certainly concept of 'psycho history' does not exhaust what EPT has done. It my be closer to ***'Hermeneutics' of History***. I still do not know what I have discovered in this essay and desperately wanting to communicate is already known to others or am struggling on the same path. But today I have decided to communicate to the readers about my insights which have fallen into my lap and which if communicated to other will yield further delight

Preamble and Articulation of Problems

"It is only when ordinary consciousness recognizes itself in Philosophical consciousness and the Latter in the former that, Psychoanalysis will be achieved, that science will be alive and ordinary Consciousness will be scientific." Jean Hyppolite. (P.165, The structruralist controversy.).

Freud the genius and mental giant of all times is identified with certain discoveries and contributions. Freud's writings have 'Unconscious' as focal point and 'Dreams' are at the centre stage of subject of his enquiry.

Over span of fifty years Freud himself viewed his works with aloofness and improvised his concepts and terminology, with vigor and internal logic. Whenever he has attempted to develop interface with other disciplines he has done so with caution, that is by developing his Auxiliary theories.

Emergence, improvisation and survival of Psychoanalysis as a discipline is fundamentally dependent upon its ability to 'interpret' human experience. and decipher the Fetishism of the Image and expression borne in the depths of the human 'unconscious'. These human experiences in the 'fetishized form', i.e. in the form of Dream images, hallucinatory images are 'communicated' to the dreamer himself in the 'realm' of consciousness. Freud was able to defetishize these images through a rigorous and critical method and technique which has become immortal in his Book "Interpretation of Dreams".

In the post Freudian age Philosophers and Historians in Europe have struggled to draw parallels between his endeavor and those of Karl Marx and G.W.F. Hegel. This exercise has passed through severe critical evaluations of Freud's works. The central themes of these debates have been, firstly comprehension of Freud's method and technique of Interpretation underpinning his founding works and secondly its compatibility and uniqueness, with reference to those deployed in philosophical sciences such as logic and phenomenology and with other human sciences such as 'History', anthropology, archeology and sociology.

Two of the most important areas of the controversies which Interpretation of dreams faced are, whether dream image is compatible with 'Language' and whether Freud's technique can be identified as compatible with research techniques, available for comprehension of human 'history'. The Essay seeks to evaluate Freud's founding work of psychoanalysis, IOD in following contexts, summed up as below.

a) The first stumbling blocks for the 'interpretation' of dream image are, 'complete lack of logic' and non – comprehensibility! Presence of 'logical relations in spoken and written languages and their absence in dream images and hence whether and how Freud dared to equate dream image with language is paradoxical and under such circumstances why and how Freud could develop such technique of interpretation? Considering Freud's statements that "The interpretation of dreams is the royal road to the knowledge of the Unconscious activities of mind", the focus of debate became what is the 'status' and 'nature' of the 'Unconscious'. This spurned up a sharp debate between two stalwarts in seventies of twentieth century, J. Lacan and Paul Ricouer regarding status of 'dreams' as equivalent of 'language' of the 'Unconscious'.

b) Secondly, till 1920. Marxism was regarded as the only contender for being called as 'Historical Science'. In the subsequent era a steady stream of 'Marxist' intellectuals migrated into Freudian camp or tried to pull out certain aspects from Freud's works to 'transplant' on to Marxist theories. However none of them (barring William Reich) has dealt with why and how Freud's theories which were built on foundations of 'Dream Images' the base station of 'incoherence' and 'anti logical expressions' can become so relevant for being termed as Historical Science?

It was Carl E. Schorske, the Marxist historian, who did not spare Freud and his founding works of Psychoanalysis- Interpretation of Dreams to rake up the issue! Freud's identification of work of psychoanalysis ... a process of revealing ... with the Sophocles tragedy 'Oedipus Rex' and his treatment of 'Hamlet' prompted Carl E. Schorske to investigate deeply into Freud's biography as a historian and measure him with the same yard sticks, with which Freud analyzed others. He appreciated Freud's method as bold and 'anti- political' however a closer glaze at Freud's work evoked him to launch a frontal attack on him in which he (Carl E. Schorske) led him to identify Psychoanalysis' as 'a- historical 'Science'.

It is noteworthy that by the turn of nineteenth century, Psychoanalysis came into existence through a concerted and prolonged struggle against massive social, cultural and political resistances and still could influence intellectuals, cultural and social life of twentieth and twenty first century. In an endeavor to become a distinct human science with its tools, techniques and method of analysis and investigation, Freud exhibited high amount of flexibility to extract and integrate number of contributions from other scientific disciplines and almost attempted to turn his theoretical edifice into critique of Religious Weltanschauung.... My Essay attempts to focus on such efforts.

If we note that as a radical student, Freud's concern was mainly focused on Hysteria, Neurosis and other psychic disorders which gripped the upcoming social orders in last four decades of nineteenth century Europe and inspired him to offer a Novel treatment which would avoid tragedies in personal lives of individuals and bring about a cure to make their life tolerable and worthwhile to live. What received Freud's paramount attention was the realm, which was regarded as completely 'solipsistic', 'psychically suppressed', and 'inaccessible' to rational thought, the realm of 'the human unconscious'. The methodology and technique of interpretation evolved and matured during his close collaboration with Joseph Breuer (Studies on Hysteria) and with his work 'A Project for Scientific Psychology'. This has been well established by Paul Ricouer's 'Freud and Philosophy' and other works. But uniqueness of Freud's method to surpass the 'solipsism' and venture into interpretations of unconscious events lies in his methodological presuppositions and tools at the disposal of the mental science, unlike those of Chemistry and Physics. Here (next segment) I have discovered what he shares with Karl Marx in approaching what we call as subject and object of Investigations.

These two debates have raised questions of very serious nature for students of History. Paul Ricouer could bring to the forefront Freudian method of archeological excavation and exploration from the realms of conscious to the realms of unconscious, in order to bring to the light the unspoken voice of the 'suppressed'. By way of confronting it with Hegelian phenomenology, ***Ricouer discovered the biggest achievement of Psychoanalysis, unavailable to Philosophy, which he identifies as its technique of interpretation***!

Exactly opposed is the view point of Carl Schorske! He found the archeological digging as totally reductive and which prevented S. Freud from offering and founding a genuine 'Historical Science!

These controversies are two serious issues for psychoanalysis and are explored in greater details in respective segments of this Essay. They are the central theme of this Essay.

What I have done in this Essay is to confront S. Freud with Paul Ricouer, who considered as Freud's contribution in developing methodological arsenals, his technique of interpretation of dream images, to work on the series of 'Condensations' and on what Freud encountered in 'remains' and 'suppressed' within dream images.

Secondly Paul Ricouer's confrontation of Freud's treatment of Sophocles's drama of Legendry 'Oedipus' and the Psychoanalytic method and technique, leads us to stumble on two fundamental questions,

a) Can Freud be identified as 'Modern Oedipus' in IOD and

b) Why Freud had to resort to interpretation of his own dreams to illustrate and develop his scientific treaties?

Paul Ricouer's Essays, particularly, from "Freud & Philosophy", remains most rigorous, Novel, and delightful Essays and his is lonely and fresh attempt to get into the depths of Freudian method and technique of interpretations (Hermeneutics).

Above two questions have become the subjects of Carl E. Schorske's Essays on Freud. This serious and rigorous attempt by this renowned Marxist Historian Carl E. Shorske, in his Essay, 'Freud and Patricide' is a very cogent and coherent argument and in this chilling debate with Freud he claims of identifying Psychoanalysis as an 'A- Historical Human Science'. This attempted enquiry penetrates through Freud's own dreams and scans through Freud's entire life and its historical context. Such a formidable attempt seemingly destroys, threatens or discards Freud's claims of 'psychoanalysis as Historical Science and reduce it to Freud's Autobiography'. .

- **Oedipus <u>Rex</u> and Hamlet**

My Essay essentially concentrates on what, where and why both these great critiques and admirers of Freud have missed, and undervalued two significant sections / chapters in IOD namely, the chapter 'Means of Representation' (of logical relations) and secondly a portion of Freud's discussions in Chapter VII, on 'laws of formation of condensation' in the mysterious phenomena called dream image!

For me both these, two important contributions add much more to Freud's technique of interpretation and his success in discovering the secrets of dream fetishism! All my efforts have been directed to extract these supreme discoveries (<u>remained unattended</u> and not appreciated fully) and to search for areas of their applications in the fields outside 'Psychoanalytic Framework, i.e. the field of Research into Human History.

This Essay is focused on expounding on the discovered laws of formation of Dream Image in Chapter VII... Discovery of **'Historical Law' of condensation and representations remains** Freud's most significant **and momentous revolutionary** discovery and has **brought Psychoanalysis close to becoming a contender for being named as a Historical science!** Through dream analysis it recovers, recaptures the historical past by interpretation of *archaic 'remains' and at the same time liberates what has suffered from condescension.. What I have attempted to focus is the centrality, significance and indispensability of understanding the concept of 'means of representations' in understanding Freud's magnum opus 'The Interpretation of Dreams'.*

Finally one must ask why this subject of 'method in Freud' has remained unattended or assigned so less an importance even by the great masters and interpreters of S. Freud? It is only Carl Shorske has addressed this topic of method very squarely. He has approached it in a typical German Way, as a dialectical relationship between subject and object of investigation. He sees a very systematic method in Freud's dealing with this scientific treaty. However he discovers Freud's 'personal plot' as the life giving substance of the treaty. The entire relevance of 'self analysis' boils down for him as 'personal plot'. I have paid sufficient attention to demonstrate the possible vulgarization implied in this attempt!

After reading and re-reading of S. Freud's Interpretation of Dreams and subsequent works I have realized that in Freud, the old conflict between Individual and social, individual and universal remained unresolved and Freud had to pay the Price for remaining 'disabled' to address his lessons and discoveries of psychoanalysis to 'humanity as such. It was painful for me and that despite Herculean efforts why he could not provide powerful impetus to human thirsts of which he discusses under his Lecture on Religious Weltanschauung...

In recent times it is psychoanalyst philosopher John Mill's book, "The unconscious Abyss" paved the way for revival of the debate on method and the epistemological and ontological questions in his anticipation of Freudian theory of the 'unconscious' in few passages of Hegel's phenomenology. If so, why Hegel missed it? But important issue for me was whether you find few loose endings in Freud which would help this generation to vigorously reopen the topics which are radical and were 'resolved once upon a time' by Karl Marx and his 'Capital'. .

Hence the specific tensions and controversies in Freud's method of enquiry and treatment as stated above remained the most absorbing concerns for me and I have attempted to review Freud's technique of dream interpretation and with reference to the rigorous debates intertwining various concepts in Freud's works. These specific tensions in his method, which I have characterized as dialectical, inspired 'Historian' in each one of the intellectuals to review Freud's works, 'Hysteria', 'Project' Interpretation' 'case studies' 'Civilization' and on literature. However the main focus was to understand whether Psychoanalysis possesses any intrinsic value by which it can be improvised as historical science. Freud's 'Auxiliary Theories' – Derivations from Philology, as I have concluded marks an impasse.

In few passages he has attempted to come close to concerns of Karl Marx, 'human work', its primitive evolution and its impact on evolution of language. Introductory Lectures and IOD (latter Editions), show Freud's great fascination in drawing   parallels between role of contraries in dream (opposite meanings) images and philological theories of evolution of symbols & language (linguistics terms with double meanings) with sundering of original identity between sexual activity and collective work of primitive man. This attempt to find resonance between two different fields and disciplines has come under ridicule from Paul Ricouer. To him, Freud's attempt appears to be an overstretched and abortive. However I have found the same attempt as bold though unsuccessful in view of his intellectual grooming and lack of comprehension of evolution of social contradictions under capitalism.

In writings subsequent to IOD Freud showed greater and greater concerns about nature of 'social groups' and history of civilization. Weaknesses of his social theories went on getting amplified. He could never come to terms with 'history of groups and modern capitalism. His attempts to come to terms with human work remained marginal and 'auxiliary' in face of the massive crisisof civilization Freud encountered.

Here we are faced with prophetic remarks by young Karl Marx, "What is to be thought of a science which remains aloof from this enormous field of Human Work"? This raises the question mark on the existence and development of Psychoanalysis as Science itself.

Here I was fortunate to come across the works of great Historian E.P. Thompson, particularly his work, 'The Making of the English Working Class' and I said to myself, here is a great work, a path breaking work which can carry forward S. Freud's discoveries, his techniques of interpretation, discoveries of sources which have suffered trans valuation and method of enquiry in the field and area of research into Human History!

(- Karl Marx & E.P. Thompson- Inspiration from Chartism)

It is well established that Psychoanalysis itself **as a critical science** sprang from maturation of capitalist (bourgeoisie) relations of production, exchange, distribution, circulation and self expansion and psychical disorders are resultant of advent of Civilization. Hence its relationship with the 'principle science', Marxism can never be ignored.

All above controversies and debates, the intellectual gains of Psychoanalysis, acquire significant moorings in works of few of the Marxist Authors. I am specifically referring to the works of one of the greatest Marxist Historian of times, Edward Palmer Thompson. But where Freud fails, **E.P. Thompson succeeded.** His treatment of the role of Methodism spanning almost seven decades in 'The Making of English Working Class' gives us an hope that Freud's gains in the most crucial area of discovering the laws of the unconscious and **application of Psychoanalysis to Interpretation of Class experiences** may finally see the 'day light' and if it is true, I think part of the credit must go to Eric Fromm's works which show clear influence on E.P. Thompson.

But such 'influences' alone could not have spurned E. P. Thompson's imagination. The story of Methodism's role, in 'making' which also could be, I suspect, has partially been spurned by 'self analyses of E. P. Thompson, the son of a Methodist Father. We cannot term the 'Making of' as a personal plot but unfolding of a long term historical tendency on part of working masses to liberate from the Oedipal guilt, which coincides with the Chartist Movement for social control! I tend to ascribe E. P. Thompson's success to his masterly working out of psychoanalytic technique in 'liberating or rescuing the 'ordinary' working men and women from the 'enormous condescension' of posterity.

E. P. Thompson's magical definition of law of History, as perpetual or 'eternal condescension of the past from the present (posterity) sounds like or parallel to S. Freud's efforts, like an archeologist, of excavating past 'remains' from the enormous weight of the posterity.

Techniques adopted by E.P. Thompson are those of 'real archeologist' or one can say that he could expand, broaden and elevate the concept of 'excavation' through developing socio- psychoanalytic technique to uncover the deeper meanings in Historical movements. And thus he has resolved Freudian paradigm of individual and social!

There also appears to be a complete identity between Freud's and E. P. Thompson's concept of condensation. E.P. Thompson's interests in photography, history and Montage provided him the improvisation of interpretative techniques which are closer to those of Freud but divergent enough to grasp dynamics internal to movement of groups and classes.

In case we conclude that E.P. Thompson has succeeded in such an integration it will open up innumerable opportunities for Psychoanalysis and Marxism both to understand and analyze phenomena which have remained beyond comprehension!

My Essay attempts to explore this.

(-Why Hegel 'missed' Psychoanalysis?)

(1) Review of Literature on Interpretation of Dreams.

Numerous attempts have been made to draw parallels between Freud, Marx and other great thinkers in modern History by Academicians. Similar attempts have been made by Marxists and by a very few Freudians to assess the significance of Freud's Theories to Marx. There are also Marxists who have been trying to incorporate various aspects of Freudian systems to coin new concepts and have achieved breakthroughs.

There are a very few who have struggled during twentieth century to discover something marvelous and of epochal value in Freud's writings and i.e. his theory of Imagination. I had read significant Portions of Freud's writings, and was disappointed since no works of Freud which I had read by that time other than his writings on aesthetical subjects had dealt systematically the role of Imagination. Subsequently works of the Surrealist Breton and importantly valuable references to Freud by Film Maker Sergei Eisenstein (The Psychology of Composition) inspired me to read seriously, the founding works of Psychoanalysis, Interpretation of Dreams. However decisive significance of it was realized after I came across works of the Marxist Historian E. P. Thompson, "The Making of the English Working Class ". Important intention in writing this Essay is to demonstrate that no other work has come so close Freud's I.O.D. and interpretations of Imagery as that of E. P. Thompson's 'The Making … ' For critiques, there is no apparent meeting ground between Sigmund Freud and E. P. Thompson except that both of them shared the concerns for 'Survival of Human Civilization'. If for E. P. Thompson it were the Nuclear Arsenals which threatened the Foundations of Civil Society, for Freud it was the untamed instincts, particularly the Sexual ones, in their unbridled striving for satisfaction, may announce the extinction of Human Race and Civilization, unless they are brought under "Self Control".

It is very difficult to bridge the yawning gap and unsurpassable barrier between the two theories regarded as poles apart. Psycho Historian **Peter Gay feels that "The worlds of psychoanalysis and of history are, and ought to remain, worlds apart". Probably he intended to differentiate between individual- solipsism, psychoanalysis deals with and waking life which remains focus of the historical science. However today we can only state that,** something like this (total insulation) was there between the Waking life and Dreaming before S. Freud swept it away, particularly when Freud's theories have been branded as 'regressive in focus', 'solipsistic', 'a - historical', 'analytical with archeological thrust' and when Freud's central discovery of 'Oedipus Complex' has been regarded as incompatible with E. P. Thompson's focus on 'working class'. ---

E.P. Thompson, on the other hand is committed to historical ascendance and progression and dialectical treatment of the subject derived from Hegelian Phenomenology.

In last three decades, Art critics, Historians, philosophers of the 'far left' and few leading from Human Science Circles have searched through Freud's Literature and the rigorous debates have led to articulation of various themes which we are about to discuss below. However none has made even a passing reference to the works of Historian E. P. Thompson, particularly his work 'The Making of the English working Class'. Nor do we find in this great works a single direct reference to Freud.

I am not aware of whether E. P. Thompson ever had read Freud. But I guess, Freud's influence has come via works of sociologist Karl Mannheim' and Erich Fromm. .Also distinctly visible is his treatment of Hysteria and psycho-pathological expressions within Methodist tradition intrinsic to the process of 'making of the working class'

After reading E.P. Thompson's 'The making… 'carefully I did conclude that the broader and long terms Historical Perspective of the classes have been articulated by him through interpretation of linguistic and cultural expressions. His demystification of ideological and political trends is derived from unique integration of Freudian interpretative technique and Marxist methodology.

The present Essay aims at review of themes articulated by leading lights like Karl E. Schorske, Paul Ricoeur and Jacques Lacan and few others in the areas of Freud's Methodology and technique of Interpretation of Images, specifically those from the human unconscious and in understanding the laws governing the Human Imagination. However it appears that they have half finished their endeavors to grasp Freud's ideas and discoveries in I.O.D., which can impact and certainly change our understanding of social imagination, mass psychology and history. It was a pleasant surprise for me to discover that in his historical works, 'The Making of....'

E. P. Thompson's has succeeded in integrating Freudian technique of interpretation of 'Human imagination' and its improvisations. My endeavor is to capture the most fascinating elements of this technique, the series of difficulties as paradoxes and contradictions involved in such an attempt of Integration and to present a new scenario born in this process.

Towards 'Unconscious Imagination'

Let me get down to the most significant peculiarities of Freud's I.O.D. Fascinating aspect of is that he is the first amongst the few to understand character of Dream Image as a Psychical structure and also the first to develop the technique of it's interpretation, with scientific method and through rigorous expounding and exploration of the laws of their generation development and translating them into intelligible language. In I.O.D. he has made considerable efforts to Review the Scientific Literature dealing with characteristics Dream Image. His review focuses on the central contradiction between characteristics of Dreaming and Waking life. He aims to discover the underlying forces, the processes beneath them and "by whose concurrent and or mutually opposing actions dreams are generated." (I.O.D. p.57-Chpt. 1).

By way of summery of literature from philosophy, classical and scientific writings, dating from antiquity to modern age, Freud has assigned following relevant and important noteworthy Characteristics of Dreams.

1. Dream lacks intelligibility and orderliness.
2. It defies all laws of conscious thinking. The thought activity in waking life takes place in Concepts as against in Images during dreaming while asleep.
3. During sleep voluntary ideas become difficult and streams of involuntary ideas arise. They lack Intentions, will and logical coherence, relations and accept the most violent contradictions.
4. Dreams show total disregard to common sense, aesthetic taste, transgress the bounds of Morality acquired and express unbridled cravings in sexual matters and reveal close affinity to madness.

5. They arise like lightning flashes but are rapidly *forgotten under the weight of conscious thought.*

The literature also brings forward few other important mutually opposing and contradictory trends determining the Phenomena of Dreaming. In sharp contrast to the modern psychiatry and theories owing allegiance to views that Somatic or Organic stimuli are chiefly responsible for governing the excitations, emotions and then the dreaming, he set out instead to deduce rules governing the occurrence of Dreams, and particularly the images pertaining to Typical Dreams. As against all other trends he emphasized the Psychical attributes of dreaming and to conclude that they have disguised meanings and function to perform.

The philosophers committed to "somatic stimuli Theory " and few others had realized the two functions of dreaming, namely giving expressions to fragments or residues of previous days, described as reproductive imagination and secondly have accepted the role

Of "Fantasy Images" arising from the depths of mind and giving expression to "something repressed"." The psychical energy which has been stored up during the day time by being inhibited and suppressed becomes the motive force for dreams at night."

(Quote from Deluge in I.O.D.p.152). ----

Only Volket had come close to ascribing dreaming a psychical function of liberating the "Productive Imagination" which is obliged to paint in pictorial forms. (Ref. p.155 I.O.D.) His insights paved Freud's way to develop theory of *Associative Imagination.* I should highlight here that *this concept provided* Freud insights to carry out 'self analysis' and emboldened him to venture into unknown dimensions of laws of Human Imagination and laws of the 'Unconscious.'

In Freud's own words, Interpretative journey begins with review of literature on dreams and the problems of dreams, but soon "merges in to more comprehensive problems, the solution of which must be approached upon the basis of material of another kind." --(I.O.D. p.57-Chpt.1).

It is my desire to grasp key footsteps in Freud's journey in to the realm of Imagination, and the area of history which he approached through radically different contours, hereto unknown, and are significant for Marxists as they converge on to the areas of Marxist concerns, such as social relation sexuality and other drives, human work & consciousness of 'ordinary' common man'. In doing so I have focused upon Freud's most controversial attempt to formulate "Auxiliary Theories" in order to address to the affinities between philology and psychoanalysis, resonance between discoveries in philological discipline, having close affinity to Freud's own concerns, such as disintegration of human sexual needs and human labor in the course of 'prehistory' and it's expressions in symbolic language.

Recently philosopher John Mill in his book, "The Unconscious Abyss" has attempted to discover Freud's theory of 'Unconscious' in few passages in Hegel's Phenomenology and the Encyclopedia of the Philosophical Sciences'. Hegel's Anticipation of Psychoanalysis' or birth of psychoanalysis in Hegelian philosophical system, particularly in the heart of Phenomenology is his endeavor.

On 'Unconscious'

Jon Mills on Hegel and Freud –'The Unconscious Abyss

"This is why Hegel is good for psychoanalysis: he provides a logic and truth to the unconscious that is internally consistent and coherent, thus capable of withstanding philosophic criticism when empirical limitations are encountered. Hegel can bring philosophical and logical rigor to psychoanalytic theory"-Jon Mills

- John Mills- Hegel, Chorcot and S. Freud.

Summery of it runs as follows.

1)Complex forms of the "psychological" would not be possible without the preservation of presentations and images in the "night like abyss" This is the area where John Mill has attempted to bring Hegel closer to the seat and birth place of Dream Images.

2) Hegel acknowledges the activity of the unconscious abyss, as limitless, infinite, and inaccessible to the conscious will.

3) For Hegel, *imagination is subordinated* to cognition as spirit recovers itself in the image. , imagination determines images, first in reproductive imagination, (as reproducing images called forth by intuition), secondly, in associative imagination, by Elevating images as representations to the level of universality, and thirdly, in phantasy, as a determinant being in the forms of symbols and signs. Hegel ultimately sees imagination through to its end.

4) Hegel points to the dialectical activity of the unconscious as 'telic' in generating its own oppositions and transcending itself within itself as sublimation. Hegel also tacitly suggests that self-awareness is born out of *such unconscious activity, thus giving the unconscious a primary role in psychic organization and conscious motivation.*

5) No longer driven by rational consciousness in its search for unity within the external world, spirit resorts back to its earlier form projecting its desires within fantasy. Perhaps on the most primitive level, spirit seeks to go to sleep once again, to return to a tensionless state and recover its lost unity with the Absolute. Therefore, the fundamental striving for unity leading to the movement of withdrawal back into the abyss is the basic structural dynamic of madness.

John Mill positions Hegel w.r.t. Freud in a way (it sounds as if Hegel speaks in Freudian language and which is regarded as archeology within phenomenology) that it is difficult to differentiate the concerns of Hegel and Psychoanalysis when he says, "Perhaps the implicitness of the abyss has been made most clear in its relation to mental illness. In reference to the role of the unconscious, Hegel's theory of mental illness has received the most attention in the literature. For Hegel, the unconscious plays a central role in the development of insanity (Wahnsinn), or more broadly conceived, mental derangement (Zerstreutheit). Hegel explains

"...the spiritually deranged person himself has a lively feeling of the contradiction between his merely subjective presentation and objectivity. He is however unable to rid himself of this presentation, and is fully intent either on actualizing it or demolishing what is actual" (p.367, Zusätz to § 408, Vol.2).

John Mills who understood, how Hegel had come so close to anticipation of Psychoanalysis does not dwell on why Hegel still missed it (unconscious). Philosopher like Paul Ricouer's first observation that Phenomenology up to Hegel had no interpretative technique to relate and decipher the Fetishism of the Image arising from depths of unconscious has significant value.

Freud himself however has made a passing casual reference to Hegel's treatment of dreams in his quote (p.120 –I.O.D.) from Spitta 'Dreams are Devoid of all objective and reasonable coherence' ***meaning that it is completely devoid of 'logic'.***

Never the less both Hegel and Freud have Imagination as the subject and object of their enquiry with an underline that it is 'Unconscious Imagination'.

In this context, the famous formulation by S. Freud, "The interpretation of dreams is the royal road to the knowledge of the Unconscious activities of mind" brings us close to the concerns of this Essay. Before we move ahead on this 'royal road' to grasp Essential elements of Freudian method let us not overlook the Paradoxes, at least their outlines, articulated by those, who studied it closely.

Setting the First Paradox – Ricouer differentiates Psychoanalysis from Phenomenology.

Above I have summarized attempt by philosopher John Mill to focus on what differentiates Hegel' phenomenology and Freud's psychoanalysis However such an exercise of discovering Psychoanalysis within Hegelian phenomenology or vice versa, meets sharp opposition from Philosophers like Paul Ricoeur. Interpretation of Dreams has been regarded by Freud himself as "insight which can be gained ones in Lifetime!" Most of the well known commentators on Freud's I.O.D. seem to be in agreement with this statement.

"A great Novel of Human culture, Human creations and expressions" have staked its claim as elaboration of Interpretative Technique of Deciphering social Hieroglyphics. Of means of Interpretation of psychical representations, to get behind the secrets of Human Existence! ", (Paul Ricouer).

Jacques Lacan, Carl Schorske and Paul Ricouer
Three Stalwarts– Pioneering Critiques of
Psychoanalysis.

(Critiques)

Out of many scholars, Paul Ricouer has extensively dealt with Philosophy of Freud and as science of Interpretation. Not coming from any Dominant movements his views is refreshing and concern Universal at the same time. "I do not believe that Freud may be confined to less Human Elements in man, but my enterprise stems from the apposite conviction; Psychoanalysis conflicts with every other global interpretation of Phenomena of Man because it is an

Interpretation of Culture". (Freud & Philosophy Ricoeur p.11). In doing so he has pitched Freudian Hermeneutic Method to Reflective philosophy and Phenomenology in particular. At the moment I intend to just set the context of the debate and not dwell upon the intricacies and details it may involve.

Now let me summarize J. Lacan and then counter pose it to Paul Ricouer's Hermeneutics.

J. Lacan, coming from the fields of Psychoanalytic Movement compares Freud's discourse with Phenomenology, to explore how Psychoanalytic discoveries assume full sense in the domain of symbolism, human Language and communications. For last few decades after ---Freud's death, J. Lacan has defended Freudian Orthodoxy by extracting Linguistic essence of the Interpretative technique and significance of concepts, "Unconscious", "Repression",' Resistance " and "Sublimation" within psychoanalytic discourse. His massive experience as psychoanalyst enabled him to discover within analytic situations the role played out by mighty forces of sexual Instincts, Oedipal desires and their cravings for Satisfaction and Expressions. ---

The relations between Psychoanalysts and -- Patients have been treated by him as a Field in which protracted conflict between Master –Slave assumes full-blown expression. This he calls as slave's 'working through' the layers of Repression (from uppermost to the bottom most layers) in which sexual Oedipal desires and their cravings (hidden and Enveloped in variety of forms) for satisfaction are expressed, intensified and projected on to the analyst during discourse. This journey from the 'day today' to the 'most primitive' expressions or articulations by patients after prolong experience enables slave to achieve symbolic and ideational expressions of his Labor. "This ardent and unique technique of interpretation and efforts (labor) of Patient give Interminable verbal expressions to the 'Material Repressed in the Psychic Depths"

Thus for Lacan, the conflicts assume cultural expressions during discourse. This ability and potential in *psychoanalytic* situations to encompass within it's discourse expression of psychic material which is on one hand, most solipsistic, ridiculous to the other hand the most enlightening and intelligible expressions prompted him to define "unconscious (which is) structured like Language". This is the evaluation of Lacan's works by Anthony Wielden who concluded that, "By defending Psychoanalysis against the onslaught of ' Ego Psychology" "Behaviorism" and " social Psychology" Jackus Lacan elevated Psychoanalysis to the level of Phenomenology".

Paul Ricoeur has viewed this exercise of elevating Psychoanalysis to the level of Phenomenology with suspicion. He warns readers about the danger of defining an unconscious that is not 'originally implicated (involved) in the inter-subjective relations remains solipsistic'. This he calls as first topography. And as against this, the second topography which proceeds as dialogue, is 'set up in the inter subjective field' and hence satisfies the requirements of phenomenology. This is because psychoanalytic dialogue works at the level of 'operational' rather than 'uttered', 'lived' than 'represented' and it's texture is not that of instinct but meanings or 'semantics' of desire.

Paul Ricoeur differentiates psychoanalysis and phenomenology on following criteria.

Firstly "Phenomenology attempts to approach the real history of desire obliquely; starting from a perceptual model of the unconscious, it gradually generalizes the model to embrace all lived or embodied meanings, meanings that are at the same time enacted in the element of language. As against this, Psychoanalysis plunges directly into the history of desire". (P. 389 F & P) Hence phenomenology is an approximation of Freudian Unconscious.

Secondly the Freudian unconscious is rendered accessible through the psychoanalytic technique of interpretation and handling resistances; but this type of <u>archeological excavation has no parallel in phenomenology</u>.

Thirdly for Phenomenology the main barrier separates the preconscious and conscious (Cs / Pcs. Ucs) while for psychoanalysis it is (Cs., Pcs / Ucs). That is, unconscious of phenomenology is the preconscious of psychoanalysis.

Fourthly in psychoanalysis remoteness and distortion separates the representations from their roots. These derivatives are ideational and affective, requiring instrument of investigation. <u>The kind of</u>

technique required to understand the remoteness and the division at the basis of the distortion and substitution that makes the text of the consciousness unrecognizable. They require concepts like dream work, displacement, condensation which belong to discipline named 'hermeneutic' and supported by complimenting 'energy' and force.

Fifthly each system, such as unconscious, is capable of cathecting representations.

Sixthly, the intersection of desire and language, accounted by archeology of the subject, require co ordination of economic language and intentional language. Lacan's attempts to elevate '*economic expressions*' to the '*linguistic concept*' status has come under severe criticism from Paul Ricouer and he terms this as disastrous. I have attempted to deal with these differences separately.

As opposed to Phenomenological approach number of authors have agreement over Freud's statement that 'Interpretation of Dreams is The Royal road to a knowledge of the unconscious activities of the mind' which can be likened with the method adopted by Archeology. Psychoanalytic technique of Interpretation of Imagery is a direct off shoot of his 'Studies of Hysteria and Psychopathology of Hysteria' jointly published by S. Freud and Joseph Breuer' . This works which approached Hysterical symptoms and Phantasies of the patients laid the foundations of technique of interpretation and method of investigation of I.O.D. Freud's journey from "Project of Scientific Psychology " (1895) concludes in I.O.D.

Freud's founding of this psycho-archeological method has been appreciated by critiques such as Anthony Wilden, Art Historian J. J. Spector, philosopher Paul Ricoeur and Marxist Historian Karl Schorske as liberation of nineteenth century Psychology from its Anatomical moorings'. They have regarded its status as 'historical' and of termed the book as "Scientific Treaty of Epochal Value". Without exception all of them comprehended, most vital and foundational 'essence' of Freud's I.O.D. as being "Self-critical" "archaeological pursuit". They have attempted to, draw close parallels between theories of Karl Marx and Sigmund Freud. Paul Ricouer's "Philosophy and Freud" has attempted to explore Freud's discovery of the Relation between 'Hidden to the shown',

(Theory of Fetishism) and grasp his technique by which Unintelligible, Inverted, Fetishised Dream imagery is translated into Intelligible and meaningful text. This he has ***characterized as Method and Technique of Demystification***.

Question of Method in 'Interpretation of Dreams'.

Freud treats the currents of thoughts and views expounded by various Scientific Authorities on nature of dreams as representing these processes. In short he treats the authorities as exponents of psychic forces and processes, the way in which Karl Marx treats the political economy. Paul Ricouer and Carl E. Schorske have dealt at length with method of enquiry. Both of them have identified Freudian endeavor as having archeological aim, of digging through the layers of repression and finally discovering the inner most seething conflict between Instinctual representations and ossified imprint of primal authority. Out of the two Carl E. Schorske has comprehensively dealt with Freud's Method of investigation and presentation.

In his Essay, Politics & Patricide in Freud's I.O.D." Schorske evaluates it for identifying its scientific status and as a personal statement of Freud. "The surface organization (of the book) is governed by its function as scientific treatise, with each chapter and section ---systematically expounding an aspect of Dreams and their interpretations .To this scientific structure, Freud explicitly subordinated the personal content of the book, designating the dreams and memories that constitute it only as a "material by which I illustrated the rules of dream interpretation." Yet a closer look reveals a second deeper structure of the work which running from one isolated dream of the author to the next, constitutes an incomplete but *autonomous SUBPLOT of personal history*. Schorke has likened it with St. Augustine weaving his confession into 'The City of God'. Schorske appears or tends to limit the essence and significance of the 'self analyses to a kind of confession of 'patricide 'committed in thought. ---

The understanding of interrelationship between IOD as scientific treaty and as 'self analysis' is crucial as I feel that in spite of being a brilliant Essay on Psychoanalysis Schorske has been lead to draw wrong conclusions. Freud is however very clear on this subject, when he states in "Preface to the second edition" of the book, that "For this book has a personal Significance for me personally-a significance which I grasped after I had completed it. It was I found, a portion of my **Own Self Analysis**, my reaction to my Father's death."

Irrespective of Schorske's revelation, in my view Freud's admission imparts new Revolutionary dimension to the nature of Psychoanalysis as science which can constitute It self only 'in and through' Self – Analysis and establish itself as a unique Discipline in Human Science in which the **educator himself is subjected to education like that of 'ordinary consciousness' before it can aspires to become scientific'. ---**

Schorske comprehends methodology of "self analysis" in following words," In the visible structure of the scientific treaties he leads his readers UPWARD, chapter by systematic chapter, to the more sophisticated reaches of psychological analysis. In the visible PERSONAL narrative he takes us DOWNWARD, dream by major dream, into the underground recesses of his own buried past." Schorke has focused his attention to the 'second quest' that 'must interest the historian' (p.184 P & P in Freud's I.O.D).

He begins with Freud's personal – professional crisis intensified and precipitated by father's death, in the wake of rising anti-Semitism during last two decades of the century. Schorke has attempted to situate the crisis in Freud's personal life in the context of unfolding socio political crisis of Austrian social democracy and the intelligentsia. In fact this great book was seen by Freud himself as stimulated by 'the death of my father'. Schorke who finds that this sub-plot articulates Freud's personal History and a confession (equivalent of self analysis).

Partially in contrast to Schorske's interpretation Freud had seen this choice of dealing with his own dreams was a scientific pre requisite and compulsion imposed by the nature of the subject and the object, of investigating a "phenomena which is free from undesirable complications owing to the added presence of Neurotic features". The dreams of his patients and psychopaths, involved unwarranted complications. This inevitably followed that he had to undertake interpretation of his own dreams and had to reveal "to the public gaze more of the intimacies of my mental life, than I liked, or than is normally necessary for any writer who is a man of science and not a poet. Such was the painful but unavoidable necessity; and I have submitted to it….." (Preface First Edition I.O.D. p.45).

It was perfectly scientific choice, like the one chosen by Karl Marx in 'Capital', to choose typical 'commodity' forms and most free from disturbing Influence to ensure the occurrence of the phenomena in its normality. Once the choice made, it was highly courageous of S. Freud to demonstrate, within dream life, the development of fundamental social-individual antagonisms from the natural laws of formation of dreams and images. Above all, like Karl Marx, for S. Freud, it was a "question of these laws themselves, of these tendencies working with iron necessity towards inevitable results" (p.19 Capital). It is necessary to deliberate on this subject specifically, however it is noteworthy that out of scientific consideration alone Freud considered subjecting his 'dream life to investigation and exposing it to public gaze', even though it was 'painful but unavoidable necessity'' Freud overlooked personal considerations and submitted his dreams to the psychoanalytic technique. Here *the subject and object of investigation was 'self'*. It is the insufficient grasp of 'subject' on part of historian like Schorke, to treat this as 'autonomous sub plot' and to loose track of the 'laws' investigated by Freud at each stage and particularly in Freud's treatment of condensation and means of representations. It is the scientific method which unfolds in I.O.D. It was Carl E. Schorske who has acknowledged the thrust and aim of this method when he identifies his method as 'archeological digging says In the order of their "presentation one becomes aware of three layers in a psycho-archeological dig, professional, political and personal. These layers also correspond loosely to phases in Freud's life, which he presents in inverse temporal order in the I.O.D. Professional one lies roughly in the present the political, in the period of youth and childhood. Deepest of all, both in time and space the personal layer leads back into Infancy and into the unconscious"(P &p IN I.O.D.). Freud's method thus encompasses three levels of Imagination as archeological digging into the 'self'.

As an Historian, Carl E. Schorske's brilliant essay " Politics and Patricide in I.O.D." attempts to copy and follow up Freud's review of 'making of' Shakespeare's 'Hamlet' in which Freud searches through Shakespeare's life and his works to interpret deepest layer of impulses in the mind of the creative writer. 'Hamlet' itself was supposed to have been created immediately after the death of his father (just like I.O.D. was created after the death of Freud's father), "that is under the immediate impact of bereavement .... Childhood feelings about his father freshly revived." Schorske's article seems to be an attempt to 'psycho-analyze' Freud. It is note worthy that the insights he developed from his search into Freud's I.O.D. and crucial role played by Freud's discovery of universal nature of "Oedipus Complex" enabled him to incorporate them in his own method of historical research of characters, Art and Culture. This is reflected in each of his essays in "Fin-De-Siecle Vienna: Politics and Culture"

One significant point to be noted is that out of numerous dreams of himself and those of his patients, Freud has chosen only five to six *dreams of his own for exhaustive treatment, analysis and for exposition of scientific concepts.* Schorske has drawn entire material of his Book from these dreams shows not only the strength and ability of Freud's method of investigation, technique and skill of interpretation to liberate and rescue the 'remains' of the past historical life, but also the nature of Dreams, their ability to weave and draw such massive material, historical details (".. a thousand threads …an Infinite combination grows"). Another fascinating historical significance is how, structures of memory and images recreating from his personal- community life are integrated into socio order and cultural political historical scenario of the emerging twentieth century Austria-Germany from this strange sources called dreams, phantasies, myths and legends. How was this achievable? *It is on the strength of the psychoanalytic technique*

Could he do it. Yes most importantly Freud' himself has attempted to make use of this technique in several of his writings on interpretation of Art, Literature and Historical characters.

Significantly we find that Freud chooses *dream image instead of Hysteria as subject of investigation. Freud has treated Dream Image as the cell Form, 'prototype' of all abnormal psychological structures,* first member of "abnormal psychical phenomena of which further members are hysterical phobias, obsessions and delusions.

It is the method of enquiry which "necessitates dream image to be understood at the first place". "Anyone who understands dreams can also grasp the psychological Mechanisms of the neurosis and psychosis. (Psychopathological interest in Psychoanalysis. –1913) For dealing with the more comprehensive problems of psychopathology or therapeutic influence the understanding exercises Freud had to take recourse to his own dreams for interpretation. The organic relation between the two is again stressed by Freud in his Preface to the second Edition of I.O.D. Freud says, "During the long years in which I have been working at the problem of Neurosis, I have often been in doubt and sometimes shaken in my conviction. At such times it has always been the I.O.D. that has given me back my certainty. It is thus a sure instinct which has led my many scientific opponents to refuse to follow me more especially on my researches upon dreams."(P.47 I.O.D.).

Necessity to begin with economic "Cell Form" to understand much more Composite and complex forms of commodities has been highlighted by Karl Marx (C-M C). This is since in the analysis of 'economic forms' neither the microscope nor chemical reagents are of use. 'It is only the force of abstraction must replace both'. So is the case with psychoanalysis in so far as its method is concerned. In "The Fetishism of commodities and the secret thereof" Marx treats the commodity as a mysterious thing. This completely hides the social character of labor .Hence Marx goes on to the analysis of phenomenal form of value, "Money". .With passage of one form into other Marx ,chapter by chapter through grasping the contradictions in 'use' and 'exchange' value goes on to expound higher determinations of "Capital". Close look however reveals entry into the deeper recesses of Value creating Labor processes.

Comparison between Techniques of analysis of S. Freud and Karl Marx, it can be noted that both of them have dealt with Phenomena which can be called as 'Fetishism' involving distortion, compounding, Inversion, turning into opposites of elements constituting the "Cell Form" of the object. Freud on one hand grasping the resultant alienation of sexual Aims and constitution of Primary repression, and K. Marx on the other hand discovered the alienation resulting from Labor process under capitalist mode of commodity production.

Carl Schorske's attempt to equate the 'sub plot' with 'self analysis' only reveals lack of understanding of 'method of abstraction and amounts to injustice.

Re-writing or Reconstruction of History

Freud sweeps away Solipsism?

John Mill introduces to us fundamental nature of 'unconscious' as being incapable of 'introspection'. "A psychoanalytic account of the unconscious in which the primacy of instinctual impulses in the form of wishes as "image" simultaneously press for expression, yet remain repressed within one's "internality" as the abyss of "inwardness," unavailable to immediate introspective self-reflection". One needs to imagine how difficult it was for Freud to develop a method which could overcome this 'unavailability'.

Freud developed a method for analysis of Dream image, to penetrate beneath the remains of the fading memories. It was the scientific compulsion which compelled Freud to dig into his own past like an archeologist does.

As "self analysis" the book I.O.D. has been a novel presentation of historical Research, a story and life history recovered not from conscious memories but from realms of mental life suppressed, forgotten and unavailable to conscious thoughts. History as was experienced , perceived, felt and comprehended but banished .The material available to work on is strange, mystical, distorted and mostly solipsistic These are cryptographic images from manifest dreams and exhibiting features similar to those of neurotic symptoms, Myths, proverbs, sayings, linguistic expressions symbols etc. But reaching out to the historically buried material demands rigorous training in technique and proficiency in usage of tools and practice in relaxation of mental repression which can enable overcoming of resistances anchored in layers after layers, into deeper realms of mental life where repression thickens, phantasies replace memories and seething forces are on alert to pull down civilized norms of expressions. The process led Freud to traverse from *seemingly solipsistic imagery to network of intelligible communications and massive gathering of social experiences in the lived life*. It is like a series of analytical sessions between 'self' as analysand and imagined 'self' as Master. From the interpretation of set of five major dreams, not only the life history of Sigmund Freud *reconstructed but also unfolds the Austro-German social life at the end of nineteenth century*.

The five dreams which have been treated exhaustively are, Irma' Injection, Uncle with Yellow Beard, Botanical Monograph, the Revolutionary Dream and Set of Rome Dreams. Out of this Irma's Injection, the specimen dream, begins almost at the top of the conical,

Inverted structure (Professional Layer), passes onward to announce his first discovery, dreams are fulfillment of desires. Discovery of dream distortion, or representation by it's opposite, Inversion is established. After a detailed recovery of psychic material or memories from contempory and youthful period enters into the ground of the fulcrum / conical structure to discover at large the Means of representations at the disposal of the Unconscious desires and instincts to stirrup the hail and forcefully appear on the surface (Manifest) of the dreams. In an interpretation of single dream Freud could demonstrate unique ability of technique of interpretation when united with a force of quest for self knowledge to recapture its own lost history appearing to be banished forever by tyrannical repression. The massive energy required by Unconscious desires for forcing a way thru into the conscious, perceptual system (Dream) is an achievement of intensities provided by visual memories 'cramped' in the Unconscious. Most significant of all abilities of the dreams discovered was the process of massive condensation of various situations, experiences, personalities and locations into very strange composite images or pictures.

BISMARCK'S DREAM

I was riding on a narrow Alpine path, precipice on the right, rocks on the left. The path grew narrower, so that the horse refused to proceed, and it was impossible to turn round or dismount, owing to lack of space. Then, with my whip in my left hand, I struck the smooth rock and called on God. The whip grew to an endless length...

(- Sigmund Freud's Dreams)

This Freud calls as the unique and highest marvelous achievement of dreams. In fact Freud calls dreams as conglomeration of several such condensations. This phenomena triggered by what Freud calls as the cathexes from 'primary process' is treated in great detail in Irma's injection and 'uncle with yellow beard' and as a separate chapter. Hence the dream which can be written in half a page, its interpretation will run 'into six, eight or dozen times". Thus Freud discovers in psychic process an <u>historical law of condensation.</u>

Highest achievement of dreams, the 'work of condensation', finds marginal value in Carl Schorske's article. S. Freud defines its origin and discovers the Processes Involved. It is the process triggered or exercised by psychical intensities and is hereto unknown to conscious thought. Though *"The direction in which condensation in dreams proceeds is determined on one hand by the rational preconscious relations between dream thoughts and on the other hand by the attraction exercised by visual memories in the Unconscious. The outcome of this activity of this condensation is the achievement of the intensities (psychical) required for forcing a way through into the perceptual systems."* (I.O.D. P.754-55).

Freud has expanded various aspects of this dialectical relationship between primary and secondary processes in this chapter. Thus dream work (condensation process) is achieved by the stripping off of the foundational relations (role played by censorship) and submitting to process of compression and desires in the Unconscious. Here Freud is using the language of force exercised by two different Psychic agencies.--- The iron necessity, its inexorable nature of this law of condensation is provided by the forces which trigger it. The Analytic resolution of compounded word "Trymethyline in Irma's Injection or 'Botanical Monograph' serving as Nodal points upon which great number of dream thoughts converge and because they had several meanings in connection with the Interpretation, led to unearthing of massive chains of dream thoughts. (Refer discussions under 'considerations of represent ability'). Similar is the interpretation of 'botanical' and 'monograph' led Freud to understand they could make entry into content of the dream because they possessed copious contacts with the majority of the dream thoughts and upon which they converged and represented many times. This dialectic and the tension residing in the 'condensation', the vectors, originating from 'preconscious' and drawn towards 'unconscious' respectively, their teleological and archeological ends are demonstrated to be existing between contest of two figures in a composite images or amalgamations.

Second dream, Uncle with yellow beard, pushes the investigation further down in the layers of memories as youth and which correspond to the latent political content of dream. By analysis of the Anti-Semitic content of dream and aggression against his own Jewish colleagues, Freud discovered the most important process, *of transforming the dream desire into its apposite,* in the manifest content of the dream.

This process was assisted and also revealed by analysis of condensation process. Analysis and delineating of the Composite image of Uncle Joseph and professor 'R'' led Freud into his childhood memories. Freud discovers this principle of Distortion down to details of the dream and every dream. The question "Why the Distortion" has led Freud to a disclosure of purposive concealment and hiding. The presence of Repression (censorship) in exercising suppression of disagreeable truths, beneath their innocent disguisement. This dream is traced back to the pathological ambition and desire of his childhood to enter into Minister's shoes. And which takes the shape of ambition to earn the Title of "Distinguished Professorship " even at the cost of displaying anti-semantic aggression against his own Jewish colleagues and Friends in the manifest content of dream. These dreams have been interpreted by Freud in great depths in **order to elaborate the concept of unconscious intention**, the role played by 'Ego' to represent unacceptable truths and purpose of dream condensation under the sway of dream censorship. Freud summarizes this in sub chapter 'wish fulfillment'. "Where as the wish from the Ucs, is able to find expression in the dream after undergoing distortions of every kind, the dominant system withdraws into wish to sleep.'(p.725, I.O.D.).

Here the resemblance between Freud's treatments of Distortion in Dreams with sub chapter in Marx's Capital ' " The Fetishism of commodities and the secret thereof', are highly astonishing. For Freud this discovery resolved the question of Interpretability of dreams. Distortion consists of Inversion or turning into its opposite is meant for concealing and not disclosing thoughts in latent content, to the thoughts lying behind the dream. The purpose is to conceal the true interpretation. Representations through distortions, expression of opposite affects, articulation of 'nonsense', are all used to repress the expression of disagreeable desires, of to suppress disagreeable truths, smiting down of dream desires particularly the sexual ones pertaining to the primary system, 'Ucs'. Hiding the true nature of desires (Sexual) responsible for production of dreams. In the series of dream wishes revealed in an interpretation, Distortion is the highest in case of the sexual desires going back to the infantile stage. They "are held back from the Pcs. (preconscious) becomes the sine qua non of repression". Freud ends his discussions in I.O.D. regarding anxiety dreams and question of psychoneurosis with the remark that "The theory of psychoneurosis asserts as an undisputable and invariable fact that only sexual wishful impulses from infancy, which have undergone repression and are thus able to furnish the motive force for the formation of psychoneurotic symptoms of every kind. It is only by reference to these sexual forces we can close the gaps that are still present in the theory of repression". (p.766 I.O.D.) Freud elaborated this revolutionary conclusion in "Theory of sexuality" and all latter theories related to crisis of civilization. It is the social characteristics of sexuality as articulated in psychoneurosis should be of interest to the Marxists. It is this theory which Freud could not have proceeded to understand the same without the theory of distortion and displacement. Dream interpretation of Botanical Monograph, steps out from a layer pertaining to recent and indifferent material into the childhood experiences.

The surge of experiences pertaining to Father-Child (son) relations and the latter Developments is the canvas for this dream interpretation. Here we encounter the socio – historical melio of 1860 to 1898 Austria -Germany. As a Child. Freud recapitulated the socio-economic history and emotional life, in brief time period of his upbringing. This dream paved the way for entry into deeper recesses thru the well known "revolutionary -- Dream." and 'Rome dreams'. Carl Shorske has dealt in details the dream, which begins with a scene of student gathering, where Freud rose with fiery outburst against obnoxious remarks of Count Thun. (Count Jaffe the student leader),the dream after exhausting the revolutionary and Political content ends up in a scene on the railway platform where he found himself in the company of a blind man. (He recognized him as his dying father). Freud held urinal to help him. (P.299-311 I.O.D.). This dream is confined to bottom most layers of the imagined conical structure and returns to the surface after explaining the absurdities of dream. The Revolutionary dream which begins with rebellion against the Aristocratic Authorities, subsuming Freud's memories of 1848 French Revolution finally ends up with recapturing the rebellion against his own Father, the Authority for infant and child.

With interpretation of Rome dreams and Revolutionary dream Freud discloses the Patricidal phantasies and childhood longings for Rome the Mother of European Culture) residing deep into the unconscious. Construction of phantasy of helping father urinate is likened by him with *Hysterical subjects who alongside the real events construct frightful and perverse imaginary events or phantasies*. Dream Interpretation ends with discovering the purpose of Absurdity in dreams. In the Reversal of Roles displayed by this Patricidal Phantasy constructed by the subversive Impulse in the Unconscious. Intellectual Vengeance on Father, to send clear and loud message to Father that "I have come to something" is the Reversal of the relations between Father and son, Master and Slave. Revolutionary dream thus is able to compound, bring together, *two sets of experiences, one from childhood, father reprimanding little Sigmund, for his bed wetting, 'the boy will come to nothing' (castration threat) and other experience from his professional frustration stemming from the raging and advancing 'anti Semitism'. Condensation of these two experiences, their superimposition (not noticed by Carl Schorske) has been treated by Freud as a Hysterical symptom*. But most importantly the dream condensed the two experiences by combining two locations in to a single location (station platform). Thus the dream was addressed to the "central antagonist" count Thun. Even Carl E. Schorske has admitted the daring and courage demonstrated by Freud in sending a clear political message to the " very real political Goliath, the incumbent minister president" and who was in charge of political affairs when the book was published. This illustration would be dealt separately, here however let me limit to Schorske's interpretation. He identifies it as Freud's Rome Neurosis. as a reaction to rising wave of 'anti – Semitism', racial prejudice and national hatred ,Freud had a choice , one ,to imitate Hannibal, the Semitic General to avenge his father against Rome which symbolized organization of catholic church.(an oedipal aggression), Second , to overcome this Rome neurosis by choosing to be a Scientist. For Carl E. Schorske Freud chooses to follow in footsteps of Winckelmann the

Great archeologist and Art Historian who ardently loved Rome as mother of European culture. While clearly appreciating the 'anti-political 'nature of psychoanalysis, Schorske claims that the last episode in the dream was a 'Flight from politics.' *It only means that latent content of the dream exhibited regression to plastic images which articulated childhood desires. "He defined his Oedipal stance in such a way as to overcome his father by realizing the liberal creed his father professed but failed to defend."* (P.191 P & C). Understanding of Freud's theory as 'reductive ---Archeology' has prompted Schorske to identify Freud's theory as 'patricide' replacing 'politics, or victory over politics, psychoanalysis overcoming history. "Politics is neutralized by counter political psychology".

What Carl Schorske terms as reductive is nothing but analytical. Here Freud is not substituting Count Thun by Freud's own father nor it is a flight from 'politics'. It is an analysis by the subject none other than Freud himself. It is the journey from unrecognized towards recognition. It is an attempt to recapitulate entire gamut of meanings, down into memnic images. It is a direct plunge into history of desire and into the derealized field of transferences through the process of suspension of conscious.

It is necessary here to state that Freud finally encounters 'Oedipal Situation' and not Oedipus! Latter Freud defines the regressions in dreams and Neurosis expressed as the result of the cathexes from the Oedipus complex, which Freud latter identified as the 'nucleus of neuroses. The Inexorable Nature of this law and its manifestations have not been comprehended by Schorske. The reactionary, regressive character of 'Oedipus Complex' and its ability to imprison the 'present' and future is of prime concern of Psychoanalysis. The interpretation of above three dreams has led Freud to understand the manifestation of 'law of patricide' working in tandem with the 'law of displacement' throughout the social life of individuals at different levels and circumstances in innumerable forms (incorrectly identified by Carl Schorske inversely as theory of 'patricide' replacing 'politics'). Its inexorable influence in shaping the events in social life of individuals has been discovered by Freud in these interpretations. For Freud psychoanalysis was a science dedicated and equipped to undertake liberation of 'present' imprisoned by 'archaic past'.

Schorske further asserts that after paying off the debts of his father as a scientific liberator, Freud ventured to draw "theoretical consequences" from his discovery of patricidal impulses, and transposed into a suitable "form " by identifying himself with the 'mythic archetype', the Oedipus. " He appropriated Oedipus Myth in such a fashion as to bring out the sexual dimensions it contains. In doing so he pushed the interpretation of

Dreams as a whole one step further down from personal infantile experience, to which he had traced, in order to expose *his political encounters to the childhood of the human race. The mythic layer is the deepest in the I.O.D. where the individual experience of the unconscious is found embedded in the universal archetypal experience of the primitive man. Here personal history joins the a-historical collective".* (P.199 P & P C.A. Schorske)

In the rest of his article Schorske has confronted 'Oedipus Rex' drama by Sophocles and Freud's treatment of the subject, i.e. neutralizing politics. Schorske's essential drive is to explore the impact of crisis of political and social disintegration at the turn of century on the life of a 'liberal scientist with faith in rational polity'. Schorske has thus asserted the following. --

a) Freud pays no attention to the fact that Oedipus was a King.

b) For Freud (like Nietzsche and other modern philosophers), Oedipus quest was a moral and intellectual one: to escape a fate and acquire self knowledge. Not so far the Greeks. Sophocles' drama Oedipus Rex is unthinkable except as res publica, with its regal

Hero motivated by political obligation: to remove the plague from Thebes.

c) Although 'Oedipus guilt 'is personal, his quest to discover it and his self punishment are a public matter and are required to restore public order. Freud's Oedipus is not a Rex, but a thinker searching for his identity and its meaning.

d) By resolving politics into personal psychological categories, he restores personal order but not public order. Dr. Freud left Thebes Languishing still under the plague of politics, while he elevated his slain father's ghost to the kingship in the dream of Hungary.

e) The Latin legend on the title page "If I cannot bend the higher powers, I shall stir up the hell' *is meant to warn those in power* and echoes Ferdinand Lassalle's brilliant pamphlets 'The Italian war and the task of Prussia' as the same also bore this title. Lassalle threatened 'those above' in political power with 'forces of national revolution'

f) Juno's subversive threats have been addressed to express his own current political anxieties and youthful political predilections. Freud's interpretation of the contents of Freud's dreams, in particular, that of Lassalle, who came to grief over a woman and Lead him to damage by his 'neurosis'. "Freud also conquers the power of his own sexual temptations by clinical understanding of neurosis". Thus Freud suggests that sex is stronger than politics, but science can control sex. Schorske claims that Freud "appropriated" Lassalle's legend, by transferring the hint of *subversion through the return of the repressed from realm of politics to that of psyche*".

g) " By reducing his own political past and present to the epi phenomenal status in relation to the primal conflict between father and son, Freud gave his fellow liberals an 'a- historical' theory of man and society, ... beyond control" (P. 203, P & P Schorske). Thus Freud who entered Winckelmann's shoes as psycho-archeologist to enter the city of Rome in 1901, finally ended up by offering 'a-historical' science.

We have dealt in detail about Freud's interpretations of dreams, which contradicts the above conclusions in following aspects.

Based on earlier part of this essay, I have following observations to make on Carl Schorske's contentions.

Firstly, Freud who began with demonstrating the yawning gap between dreams and waking life finally, sweeps away the difference through a method and Technique of interpretation, by translating the 'transcript' or 'Hieroglyphs' into a mode of expression perfectly meaningful and intelligible. For Freud, '*whose characters and syntactic laws it is our business to discover by comparing the original and the translation'* In doing so the method 'works' on condensations, distortions and displacements (which are all depositories of social history, within personal psychi and pervading every nook and corner of psychic life of individual. Through analysis and interpretation of Revolutionary ***Dream Freud drew another inference (p.312 IOD) that 'they include several wish-fulfillments one along the other; but a succession of meanings or wish-fulfillments may be superimposed (arranged in superimposed layers) on one another, the bottom one being the fulfillment of a wish dating from the earliest childhood".*** **I will prefer to say that S. Freud discovered Historical Law of Condensation and Overdetermination, of Present by the Archaic Past.** This law inexorably works with force to override the barriers Posed and created by Human Development through work and Labor of centuries. This law works in exactly opposite direction that of historical development of civil society. Hence the work to disentangle the meanings from the mutilations they undergo down to details cannot be termed as 'personal categories', they are social, historical categories. The revolutionary message is that neutralizing the influence of this 'law of patricide' is necessary and hence essential to ensure the prevention of collapse of civilization and work. This gives Freud's <u>method and technique</u> a unique potential and ability to work on unconscious imagery to earn the title of, potentially, a Historical science or a science, which has ability to reclaims the historical truths or can be improvised in recapturing elements of lost history.

Secondly, I.O.D., the most significant works of Freud has led us to understand the 'social character of forces of sexuality', articulated and expressed as 'psychoneurosis' which in historical terms poses the highest threat to civilization. Particularly when instincts refuse to be diverted from their sexual aims to those of socially higher (sublimated through Human work to join the work of civilization). Freud's concept *of sublimation has implicit relationship between sexual forces and human labor.* "Society believes that no greater threat to civilization could arise than if the sexual instincts were to be 'liberated and returned to their original aim' for this reason society does not wish to be reminded of this precarious portion of its foundations". ---

Trajectory of Freud's works makes it clear that the 'return of the repressed' from politics to that of psyche, and "If I cannot ... shake the foundations" *have been intended to picture the efforts of the repressed instinctual impulses, and the frightful consequences and their menacing capacity to threaten the civilization.* Thus Juno's subversive threats have not been used by S. Freud to challenge those in power with unleashing of destructive impulses *but to highlight exactly opposite of that, i.e. addressed to Humanity and the and to scientific culture prevalent to understand the significance of a discovery of social character of sexuality.* In both the cases Schorske's apprehensions and judgments appear to be misplaced and derailed. War neurosis & associated mass phobias of 1914-17 and rise of Fascism, both have brought about social character of forces sexuality amidst the crisis of capitalism long ago discovered by him in the simplest cell form of dream image.

NAZI BOOK BURNINGS AND
THE AMERICAN RESPONSE

Thirdly, Schorske's in his treatment of Oedipus says "Freud takes a step further downward from 'personal infantile' experience into the "childhood of the human race". Again a misunderstanding has crept in. True that Freud enters into the 'ground work' in his chapter on 'Typical dreams'. But have two distinct aims but a single theme. Oedipus has been treated as part of typical dreams. Once Freud discovered the laws of formation of dream image, he grasps these tendencies (*social characteristic of forces of sexuality*) as manifesting themselves through the typical dreams' in dreams of each one of us. Second aim is to understand transformation of dream form into 'Hysteria' or Psycho Neurosis. Hence he confronts the Legend and the drama Oedipus Rex" from classical antiquity to Shakespeare's Hamlet. Freud identifies the changed treatment of the same material in "two widely separated epochs of civilization". The secular advance of repression in the life of the mankind lends the drama in which child's wishful phantasized desires, are not brought into open and realized as it would be in case of a dream. It remains repressed as in case of neurosis. The theme has been taken up for discussion separately. In a single sweep Freud has comprehended and treated, both, the 'primal' and the 'most modern' epochs at one end and as 'scientific treaty' and as 'self analysis' at other end. While copying and appropriating the 'rational' in Freud's treatment of Shakespeare's Hamlet and showing insights into Freud's methodology Carl E. Schorske, simultaneously, has articulated his prejudices as well.

There cannot be any commentary better than that of Anthony Wilden's comments on J. Lacan's 'Speech and Language in Psychoanalysis, to reply Schorske's prejudices. Wilden is able to identify analytical discourse as 'crisis of solipsism' and break up of 'repression' and "liberation of word." "I.O.D is fundamentally a thorough critique of solipsistic psychology originated by modern bourgeois world". Anthony Wilden characterizes self analysis of I.O.D, in which "subject addresses a discourse imaginary to the analyst, who is not there, has finally resulted into explosion and *final demise of solipsistic individualism*, Freud inherited from 19th century". He goes on to say that the dream which is certainly addressed to someone, it is part of Human discourse, which although expressed Intrasubjectivity, will also be expressed intersubjectively." (P.268-Speech and Language) Hence value of Lacan's works lies in " Giving us wherewithal to brush away the last vestiges of the atomistic ,linear and essentially solipsistic psychology inherited by the modern world , and replace it by analysis of relationships ,dialectical appositions and communications."(P.310 Speech and language.)

In this segment we have dealt with how technique of interpretation is exercised by S. Freud, exactly in opposition to Dream work in order to discover various laws of Dream formation. The discovery of law of condensation in association with those of distortion and displacement signifies that the method of I.O.D. can be appropriated for the benefit of interpretation of Social Imagery, frozen and fossilized, specifically in the context of 'associative imagination'. Carl Schorske's efforts to psychoanalyze S. Freud, in the context of the socio historical analysis of Austrian cultural milieu, he has ignored the valuable core of Freud's research method. My effort is to rescue the interpretative technique and method of handling resistances, for the benefit of historians. The intensive and extensive usage and validation of theses in interpretative technique in E. P. Thompson's 'The Making ...' has become my important endeavor.

Psychoanalysis -The theory of Language

In Chapter 2: 'Energetics and Hermeneutics in The Interpretation of Dreams' Paul Ricouer confronts with S. Freud's analogy or comparison of interpretation of manifest content of the dream and arriving at the latent content of the dream (dream thoughts) by way of synthesis with two texts, i.e. translation from one language to another. Same is with analogy with picture puzzle or rebus, which is something like a relation between obscure text to clear text.

He begins with Freud's concept of dream work which is inverse of analyst's work of deciphering. Ricouer reads Chapter VI of IOD to articulate how Freud deals with two main processes, condensation and displacement and how latent content transfer their 'psychical intensities' to the manifest content. He says these two processes attest on the plain of meaning, to an "overdetermination"(which means represented many times over) which calls for interpretation. (P. 93 Freud & Philosophy- Paul Ricouer).

He says further, "Overdetermination also governs, though in different ways, condensation and displacement. ----- But displacement which concerns psychical intensities rather than number of ideas also requires overdetermination: to create new values, to displace interests, to disregard the point of intensity, displacement must follow the path of overdetermination. ----- But this overdetermination, stated in the language of meaning, is the counterpart of processes stated in the language of force: condensation; displacement means transference of forces:"

It appears that Paul Ricouer considers 'Law of Overdetermination' as over riding law of creation of dream images and synthesizing following laws.

Law of Condensation
Law of Displacement and Transvaluation
Law of Representation

However as I have stated Freud's approach to over-determination is radically different than Paul Ricouer's when he says "*The direction in which condensation in dreams proceeds is determined on one hand by the rational preconscious relations between dream thoughts and on the other hand by the attraction exercised by visual memories in the Unconscious. The outcome of this activity of this condensation is the achievement of the intensities (psychical) required for forcing a way through into the perceptual systems.*" (I.O.D. P.754-55).

Hence I will concentrate on Freud's discovery of three laws- of Condensation, Transvaluation and Representation, which finds marginal value in Carl Schorske and not focused by Paul Ricouer.

(a) Focus of the debate (Absence of Logic).

I have stated above that next segment is dedicated to answer the question, 'whether Psychoanalysis is equipped to undertake liberation of 'present' imprisoned by 'archaic past' (regression) debarred from becoming conscious. 'Dream like states' reveal the presence of Unconscious with their peculiarities to 'appear' and interpretation provides it the way to make it intelligible. Without going into fineries I must state that the question cannot be answered unless, we deal properly with at least two (temporal i.e. return to older psychical structures and formal i.e. recourse to 'primitive methods of expressions and representations' in place of normal-usual ones) out of three types of regressions peculiar to dream images. Let us leave aside, the third (topographical), regression. Even though in Freud's opinion all 'the three are one at the bottom or occur together as a rule' (I.O.D. p.699).

Lacan as well as Ricouer have addressed these regressions in dream image at the level of 'language of the repressed unconsciouses. Three important modes or aspects of phenomena of psychical regression have been caused by or are the products of 'estrangement' or 'alienation' suffered by Desires and instincts imposed by (I would like to identify as) '*conditions of enslavements*'. Presence of these is elaborated below. Freudian method and technique of Interpretation are pitched against and have to work in opposition to these conditions responsible for regressions. Let us understand the specific characteristics of dream image highlighted by Ricouer which rules out it's identification with Language and why J. Lacan's attempt to elevate Psychoanalysis to the status of Phenomenology of Language has come under severe criticism from him.

Lacan's immense Psychoanalytic experience of the "Human Unconscious" emboldened him to draw and embarks upon inherent potentials within Psychoanalysis to transcend solipsism and give it the status of language. I will call such an attempt as 'Auxiliary Theory'. For the of philosophers like Ricoeur, such ventures & attempts to transcend solipsistic psychology are bold nevertheless they are paradoxical to basic Psychoanalytic discovery that there is a bar between 'Ucs' and 'Pcs', created by primary repression and assigning language status to the expressions like in dream image which lacks "phonemic articulation, a semantic articulation and syntax" and hence is disastrous . Ricouer remarks, "In the first place it is impossible make the ***absence of logic in dreams***, their ignorance of "NO", makes it impossible to accord it the state of real language". He continues, "Freud once tried to do this without success, in his essay on "The Antithetical Meaning of Primal Words", it is impossible to make the archaism of Process of distortion and pictorial representation to coincide with a primitive form of language....". He quotes Benveniste saying, Freudian archaic "is such only in relation to that which deforms or represses it" (p. 397 P & P). **Any ventures to transplant psychoanalytic discoveries on other disciplines are likely to be disastrous if they happen to close the paths for emergence of new insights.**

I feel that Ricouer should have **delineated *two distinct strands in Chapter VI, The Dream Work*** of I.O.D. before drawing conclusion concerning 'the absence of logic' and 'ignorance of "NO" 'to counter 'linguistic interpretation'. In the First Edition of the dream book long and well before confronting and assimilating the ventures of Philology (Footnote 1925) , Freud had already had a fully developed technique of interpretation of Symbolism residing in 'UCS' . His treatment of Schrener's symbolic interpretations, and those pre-instituted symbols and readily available and used by dreams from other sources and are dealt separately under sub-segments 'c' and 'd' of this essay below. Here I would like to highlight that I have dealt with this issue elsewhere in this essay. I have brought out the significance of these two insertions in Interpretation of Dreams, made in 1909 and 1912. "The Antithetical Meanings of the Primal words', passages from Karl Abel's essays, are the addendums to the chapter dealing with symbolism and this has been developed by Freud as Hypotheses or Auxiliary theories. Hence I have refrained here from referring to any of these addendums. Instead I have dealt with this subject under sub segment 'Freud's Auxiliary Theories … '

Freud's or J. Lacan's attempt to assign the status of language to dreams or to the structure of the Unconscious, cannot be understood in face of this 'the absence of logic' unless we recap the contributions of his Methodology and technique which enabled him to draw out the *laws of formation of dream image, of the law, governing the Phenomena, it's origins*, it's movement, development and it's manifestations in everyday life. This makes it essential for us to have more systematic view of his technique and method.

"What had already been discovered (Law, order and connections), in the formation of Dreams is operative everywhere -psychical Conflicts, the repression of certain instinctual impulses… The accompanying processes of condensation and displacement so familiar to us in dreams are also to be found everywhere" (I.O.D p.). Here, in this case also, Self Analysis favorably places Freud in the seat of common consciousness.

Freud's search of method of "Self observation "to enable him to make experiment of how far self analysis takes him to unravel the mysteries of Dream life. He makes a fervent appeal to the readers to plunge into it and accompany him in the voyage of deciphering hidden meanings of dreams Method adopted in 'self-analysis' which provided Freud additional *empathy with the analizand during psychoanalytic session*, of freeing oneself from the resistance anchored in repression. The critical faculties exercising Repressive censorship on ideas and desires in the depths of the Unconscious, "which rush into consciousness in pell-mell."

Dream is a mysterious thing, Phenomena, appearing as conglomeration, bringing together, of irrelevant images which are strange and meaningless. Strangeness arises out of "Distortion and enormous condensation" that they have been subjected to, in the Expression of their Meaning. Their Absurdity is Deliberate and expression derision, ridicule and contradiction." By way of process of interpretation of expressed content, we are led to the Latent dream thoughts, which are represented by it. They are no longer "Strange, incoherent or absurd; they are completely valid constituents of our waking thoughts."

This process runs opposite to what Freud calls "Dream Work", the work of transforming Dream thoughts into manifest content." It is this dream work that brings about the distortion which makes the dream thoughts unrecognizable in the content of the dream."

"The process of this kind hitherto has been unknown to psychology." and the novel processes such as Condensation and Displacement have never been encountered in waking life. This process of (Inversion &Representation by it's opposite) and condensation is brought about through Dream Work and I would call it *'fetishism of Image'*. This dream work derives its compromise status due Pcs as well as Ucs. Dream desires are able to force their way into preconscious in spite of censorship and primary repression.

The laws of formation of these Images are discussed most precisely in chapter, "Means of Representation ". J. Lacan seems to have derived its inspiration (Even though he has not specified it anywhere.), from this chapter. Ricouer on the other hand gives --- more stress on chapter "Considerations of represent ability" and has almost side stepped the chapter on 'means of representation. He argues, elements of dream image (representations) are not correlated through any logical relations, which is the hallmark of organized intentional Language. Primary repression to be inadmissible to consciousness. ---

There are very precise statements from Freud which offer validity to claims of Paul Ricouer. "If we reflect that the means of representation in dreams are principally visual images and not words, we shall see that it is more appropriate to compare dreams with a system of writing than with a language, In fact Interpretation of dreams is completely analogous to the decipherment of an ancient pictographic script such as Egyptian hieroglyphics. In both cases there are certain elements which are not intended to be interpreted (or read) but are only designed to serve as 'determinative...finds a parallel in these Ancient systems of writings"? (Claims of Psychoanalysis p.42.).

However immediately Freud contradicts this statement, "The language of dreams may be looked upon as the method by which Unconscious Mental activity expresses itself. *But unconscious speaks more than one Dialect.* According to the different psychological conditions governing the various forms of Neuroses, we find regular modifications in the way in which unconscious mental impulses are expressed."(Claims of Psychoanalysis, p.42-23). Ricouer and Lacan, both are vigorously engaged in articulating the vibrant conflict between dreaming and waking life at the level of 'nascent' or 'potential' but incomprehensible and incoherent because of the 'bar' created by Repression. With his hypotheses,"unconscious structured like language, and where the 'spoken word' struggles for emancipation from its status of *'deconstructed imagery'* Lacan was able to place this issue high on the agenda of debate on psychoanalysis and linguistics. Recouer agrees, "But what is specific in the psychoanalytic discovery is that language itself works at the pictorial level. This discovery is not only a call for an appropriate theory of the imagination, but a decisive contribution to it…"

But does this mean that S. Freud has accepted absence of logic as final characteristics of dream image and dream work?

(b) Primary Repression and inexpressible language. Economic Language.

Discussion on this subject can be advanced after attending to the concluding studies by Paul Ricouer. At the outset Ricouer states

1)" Freud invites us to look to dreams themselves for the various relationships between desire and language,"

2),"analysis attempts to substitute for this text another text that could be called the ***primitive speech*** of the desire."

3) Thus analysis moves from one meaning to another meaning; it is not the desires that are placed at the center of analysis, but their language."

Paul Ricouer bravely and with rigor has defended his above position in all Essays of "Freud and Philosophy." His attempts are aimed at sharp demarcation between Phenomenology of language and Psychoanalysis which runs on edge of the razor's blade .Ricouer presses Alarm bells in opposition to attempts to put dream text at the level of Language as that has been attempted by J. Lacan. ***"This is since Interpretative Technique cannot eliminate "energy concepts in favor of Linguistics "(P.367, F & P)***

Ricouer's attempt in this regard is to defend the Archeology of the subject, and to demarcate the ***economic language*** (Imagery) from the ***Intentional Language (Word)***. In imagery Instinctual drives are represented and not exactly the Desire! For him the gap between Phenomenology of Language and Psychoanalysis is obliterated by linguistic concept and co-opted by Ordinary organized Language. Since system of Repression and other mechanisms which separates Unconscious from conscious ***makes desires of unconscious inaccessible to Phenomenology.*** According to him Linguistic and Energy discourse implicit in Freudian Psychoanalytic situations are well defined, Distinct, irreplaceable even though inseparable. Hence Freud does not take Language into consideration when he treats of the Unconscious but rather restricts its role to the preconscious and conscious." (P.398 F & P).

His insight into psychoanalytic discovery that "language itself works at the pictorial level" is highly important but how far he has gone into merits of Freudian discoveries before calling for "not only the appropriate theory of Imagination but decisive contribution to it..." Following sections are an attempt towards summarizing it.

Rocoeur has provided few distinctions of dream image as being "supra-linguistics" or "infra –linguistics". He says," In conclusion, the linguistic interpretation has the merit of raising all the Phenomena of the primary process and repression to the rank of language."But the distortion, concealing, inversion which are encountered and handled during analysis are part of **Energy discourse and where phenomenology cannot lay any claims** of achievement. It is here that the intersubjectivity of Phenomenology and psychoanalysis widely differ. In a truly brilliant differentiation, he says, ," The analytic relationship may be regarded as a privilege example of intersubjective relations and ---takes the specific form of transference ......yet it is precisely here that psychoanalysis is radically distinct from anything which phenomenology can *understand and produce with it's sole source of reflection The difference is solely summed-up in a word. "Psychoanalysis is an arduous technique learned by diligent exercise and practice"*.

I think Ricouer's differentiation between Phenomenology and Psychoanalysis also answers my question raised above. "John Mills who understood, how Hegel had come so close to anticipation of Psychoanalysis does not dwell on why Hegel still missed it (unconscious)".

Ricouer continues one cannot overestimate the amazing audacity of this discovery, namely treating the intersubjective relationship as technique." (P406 F & P). The technique is broken down into three ideas.1)Analytic procedure or work ,from start to finish.2) The work of analysand another work of getting insights into his self, thus "Analysis of Self" and 3) the third form of work ,of which patient was unaware of, the mechanisms of Neurosis." "**Thus interpretation is subordinated to analytic technique of handling repression** and Resistance." In doing so Riecoer has appropriately assigned to Psychoanalysis (analytical technique) in birth of language which *remainsinexpressible* owing to repression. Interpretation has to 'work' on the specific characteristics of repression by translating its impact which perpetuates Solipsism. Hence for ordinary consciousness, the central instigator of 'dream image ' finally remains the prisoner of solipsism as a result of the bar between 'UCS' and 'PCS'.

(c) Winckelmann Vs Francis Galton.
(Law of manifestation of dream image)
(James Sally's Personality Model)

Carl Schorske's identification of S. Freud's aims with those of archeologist Johann Joachim Winckelamnn can be comprehended in right perspective if we have closer look at Freudian technique of interpretation of dream image.

I have already stated, that 'self analysis' is the life giving substance of Freudian science of interpretation. Recourse to 'Self-Analysis' enabled him to <u>discover and illuminate the technique of handling resistance and repression.</u> Also subordination of the technique of Interpretation to technique of <u>handling resistances and repression</u> also meant for Freud to subordinate linguistic discourse to energy discourse. Freud's subordination of technique of interpretation of the 'representations in dreams' to conditions of human expressions is significant, since it clearly marks the role of self- analysis which has to work against the insurmountable force of repression. I am referring to the Chapter' The Means of Representation, least paid attention to by both, Ricouer and Carl E. Schorske. Both of them have shown limited interest in Freud's exploration of the 'laws' of articulation and construction of dream images constructed from ruins of child hood memories and material.

Thanks to writings of innumerable intellectuals who have regarded Freud's theory of condensation (which may include formal, temporal or topographical regressions) as most valuable contribution to history of scientific thought. The mechanisms of Distortion and condensation are complimentary to each other. Through these mechanisms, and repressive agencies camouflage, transforms or transpose the latent dream thoughts into unintelligible, absurd text. Interpretative technique has to work in reverse, as invincible *discourse of force to achieve emancipation of meaning.* Schorske and Ricouer, both of them held absolutely different appraisals of Freud's I.O.D. and in spite of it both of them have termed Freud as a *psycho-archeologist.* It is cent percent correct to say that Freud's method of enquiry progresses like that of an psycho- archeologist, to find out what is happening at the bottom (like Oedipus violently struggling to strangle his father), but in the course of presentation it reconstructs the process by which the object, composite structure (Dream Image), makes appearance at the top surface, at the symptomatic level. Freud's job in interpreting a dream does not end up by reaching to and collecting the dream thoughts which forms the dream, "but to reconstruct from them the process by which the dream was formed, i.e. completing the <u>dream analysis through dream synthesis</u>". (p. 420 I.O.D.). Regression has to be understood through progression. Hence in the style of Karl Marx, Freud says that it is job of science to discover how <u>these laws manifest themselves with iron necessity</u>.

Freud's concept of man and personality was closer to that of his 'almost' contemporary psychologist, J. Sully (see S. Freud's inference from analysis of his Revolutionary Dream above) from, and not so much, to the archeologist, Winckellmann, as claimed by Carl Schorske. James Sully says, "Now our dreams are means of conserving these successive earlier personalities. When asleep we go back to the old ways of looking at things and of feeling about them to impulses and activities which long ago dominated us."(I.O.D.p.126 & 749). Or, "Dreams disclose beneath its worthless surface characters, traces of an old and precious Communication" (p.215-6 I.O.D.). Such a model, (I have called it a conical shaped, concentric but with no ending.), allows Freud to carefully investigate the dreams which are conglomerates of condensations, distortions and They arise out of conflict between two agencies, namely between repression and unconscious, Distortion consists of Inversion or turning into opposite, while condensation on the other hand prefers depositing of elements which occur several times to create composite figures or structures in such a way as to hide behind the recent-current events.

The desires and events going back to the childhood sexual desires are totally obliterated. This center-point of dream thoughts *becomes transitory element and is completely overshadowed and dominated by more powerful images from recent times.* This process *of condescension by the recent event also works simultaneously with condensation*! Hence Freud grasps condensation or Compression as discourse of repressive Force or Energy.

Dream -work facilitates Hallucinatory representation and revival of scenes or fantasies from childhood. *Freud developed and exercised a unique interpretative technique to de-link two distinct processes working simultaneously. One regressing from powerful images from recent times to the most ancient images residing in Unconscious System. The second one, images triggered by 'instincts' and 'desires' from numerous psychic locations simultaneously rising progressively upward thru stages, thus unifying, with the most recent or contemporary figures, locations or situations*. Analytical differentiation of these two processes, regression and progression was not possible **without improvisation and integration of Photographic technique used by Francis Galton.**

The technique to working upon this phenomenon of condensation, a psychical act can be called as Freud's radical improvisation of technique devised by scientist none other than Darwinist and photographer Francis Galton (who used the technique for identification of criminals and for racial ends). With this improvisation, Freud almost pioneered *'Montage' technique*, which latter on was adopted by by Sergi Esenstein and others. If we concentrate on the achievements Freud could make through experimental model of Francis Galton, we will realize why both, Schorske and Paul Ricouer have remained silent on it. Let me summarize Galton's role in shaping Freud's technique of Interpretation. In I.O.D. we find two clear and different reference sources of Freud's inspirations.

First one is "Weavers masterpiece."(Goethe. Faust, Part 1.) The factory of thought ,in which thousands of unseen dream Thoughts are woven and converge to form the Nodal Points unifying several meanings.

(– Botanical Monograph- Nodal Points)

Second being the most important, from the field of photography .Darwinist, F. Galton who devised technique of creating composite image by superimposing several faces from a family on the same plate to bring about the likeness and leading to cancellation (Suppression) of those features which do not fit in with the others.

Freud has considered his technique similar to that of **Galton's technique as fundamental to Dream interpretation**. In developing and revolutionizing this technique "what I did was to adopt the procedure, by means of which Galton produced composite Photographs."(P. 400 I.O.D.) As we have seen, Freud defines his method of interpretation not merely as Analytical in reaching out to dream thoughts but then "to collect the dream thoughts Which I have discovered, and to reconstruct from them the process by which the dream was formed, in other to complete the dream analysis by way of dream synthesis." (P.420 I.O.D.) . Excessive condensation and condescension (which I will discuss separately as *Freud's concept of Trans Valuation) are* thus two simultaneous processes at work in the making of the dream image. Freud demonstrate the use and application of Galton's modern photographic technique in detail in his dream of Uncle Joseph.) Ref. P219-20 IOD). *Radical improvisation of Galton's technique could allow Freud to show*

The _unconscious intentionality_ *(phenomenological)* _and_
regression to be simultaneous processes at Work. In this procedure
Galton's discoveries proved to be the mile stones in deciphering
(1) Dream distortion or inversion
(2) Dream displacement and
(3) Condensation or compression facilitated by both,
repression and instigated by UCS

Freud *has re-acknowledged this further when he discusses*
the contributions from F.Galton, under the chapter "Means of
Representation. In analysis of dream images which are composed
of amalgamation (Fusion- composite images), condensation and
condescension, S. Freud utilized the photographic technique of
Francis Galton. However in doing so he did not confine himself
to analysis of visual images alone. He turned his enterprise into,
firstly, analysis and grasp of fundamental psychical processes whose
interactions results into birth of this phenomena and secondly, *into*
how this is subjected to discovered 'laws of unconscious'.

Freud's developed his own special brand of archeology, which
compounded Galton's visual analysis and discoveries of Philology
(which I will deal with latter) are both re-casted and molded as
integral parts of his techniques.

What was Freud's achievement? To establish the 'logical and
historical' relationships existing in the network of dream thoughts
mutilated by force of repression but represented by few contesting
images. Thus the Interpretative technique has to work and undertake
a discourse which is opposite to that of dream work. This condensation
of the present images on to the past, bottom most, 'phantasies' as two
processes of superimposition and compression was discovered as a
fundamental overriding law / rule by Freud. As I have pointed out
Freud could *find a tension between images, composing the 'Fabric of*
the Dream', along the lines of historical chronological ascendancy
and topographical regression, remains one of the most fascinating
and absorbing discovery. This fully corroborates what I have claimed
earlier that, through grasp of dialectic intrinsic to condensation, that
in spite of Historical law of condensation and condescension, the
meanings jammed and debarred from expression can be liberated
and recaptured. Galton's technique after improvisation enabled Freud

to do it. I will call this as inexorable dialectical law of representation of images.

Galton's discoveries helped Freud to 'Kill seven flies in a single stroke'. Apart from Freud, Galton's insight has also helped the revolutionary Film maker-director Sergi Eisenstein, following the footsteps of Freud, in developing his famous Film technique coined as 'Montage'. By restructuring crucial contributions of S. Freud and F. Galton's work.

I have no intention to transgress the limits of this essay (which is fully restricted to Interpretation of Dreams and its ramifications) and indulge into areas beyond the scope. However I will like to illustrate it as passing remark regarding application of **Montage technique.** In applications of the techniques to visual Arts, like that of sculptures we have outstanding illustrations like that of Freud's Moses of Michelangelo. The Moses of Michelangelo not only affected Sigmund Freud but also inspired him to focus on the analysis of the postures. Freud's analysis of the seriality of events which led to the final posture under our consideration is fully '**cinematic sequencing**' of emotions and postures. Like a highly skilled archeologist and an historian he has reconstructed the 'imagined' events, by subjecting the process to the 'laws of Unconscious' discovered.

Passage from Freud's interpretation of Michelangelo's Moses is a superb illustration of the Montage technique "will neither leap nor cast the Tables from him. What we see before us is not the inception of a violent action but the *remains* of a movement that has already taken place. In his first transport of the fury Moses desired to act, to spring up and take vengeance and forget the tables; but he was overcome by temptation, and he will now remain seated and still in his *frozen wrath* and his pain mingled with contempt". One cannot have a better illustration of Galton's influence on his interpretative technique!

After assessment of contributions based on improvisation of Galton's work, now we may reach closer to the debates on Freud's archeology and on language. Dreams are formed overnight or formed over days together, but the watchful censorship exercised by Repression mercilessly achieve break up of all logical relations between dream thoughts. On the other hand unconscious exercises it's compulsion to represent the various portions of dream thoughts by combining them into a single unity. This necessity and the force acts like midwife in the birth of Dream Image. Here lies the significance of Galton's work in photography. Thus closer look at Freud's technique reveals that Freud could successfully articulate the integration of *two techniques, Francis Galton and J. J. Winckelmann which represent two sides of same coin*. Paul Ricouer has latter attempted to partially comprehend Freud's technique as 'supra linguistic' and 'infra linguistic'.

(d) Representation of logical Relations

Under sub chapter 'Primal repression and inexpressible language' I have categorically stated Freud's loud statement that dreams show total disregard for representation of logical relations. Now it is time for us to discuss it's postscript with refutation of this assertion! I have dealt with 'Question of Method' of presentation and interpretation of dreams, which has raised the paramount question 'How and what way dreams represent the 'archaic', 'childhood' and 'repressed' desires and thoughts. Or what are the means at the disposal of dreams to 'represent them' and which Freud could interpret? In order to answer these questions I have discussed what are the elements which compose Freudian technique to grasp two simultaneous processes at work. In this regard I can ask whether there is 'Galton- Winckelmann combine' in Freud which can rescue us from this impasse.

After interpretation of dream, Freud realized that "different portions of this complicated structure stand, of course' in the most logical relations to one another". 'Dream work' plays a double role, a double game; of very rapidly consolidating the mass of dream thoughts into condensed images and at the same time destroy all the logical relations and connections. Freud is candid in stating that, "The restoration of the connections which the <u>dream work has destroyed is the task which has to be performed by the interpretative</u> process". The significance of Freud's focused efforts to rescue the latent dream thoughts and relations, from the destructive onslaught of dream work, or rather that of the censorship' on dream thoughts, was possible only due to his working through the **'representation of logical relations'**. The interpretative process works on *condensations and enormous* *condescension (Trans-valuation- See latter sub chapter)* carried out by dream work.

Chapters "The means of Representation" and "considerations of representability" have a special place in I.O.D. As they are intended to picture the 'means' adopted by the repressed instincts and sexual desires to force their way into the consciousness. Freud, who had categorically denied linguistic status to the discourse of unconscious, finds parallels between Dreams and paintings.

- Representation of Logical Relations

"But just as art of painting eventually. found a way of expressing ,by meanings other than floating labels , at least the *Intensions of the words the personages represented* -affections, threats, warnings, and so on.. So to there is a possible means by which dreams can take account of **some of the logical relations** between dream thoughts, by making appropriate modifications in the method of representation" I.O.D. (p.424).

Freud further discusses in details various logical relations preferred by dreams for representation, such as, Causal relations, and, unification to represent "contraries and contradictions" .However for Most of the occasions they make use of 'Reversal' to represent contraries and contradictions. Number of times Reversals are used to represent Homosexual or bi sexual impulses. These are specific ways of carrying through Dream Distortion. Freud has used images from Goethe's poems to illuminate how contraries, of sexual innocence and desires-passions are represented in composite images

But most important logical relations highly "favored by it are *Relation of similarity, Consonance, and approximation* – the relation of "just as". Unlike any other this relation, is capable of being represented in dreams in variety of ways. Parallels or instances of 'just as' inherent in the material of dream thoughts constitutes the first foundation for the construction of a dream ; and no inconsiderable part of the dream work consist in creating fresh parallels where those which are already present cannot find their way into the dream owing to censorship imposed by resistance. The representation of the relation of similarity is assisted by tendency of dream work towards condensation." (I.O.D. Freud p.431)

Representation of Similarity led Freud to develop two important concepts. *Identification and composition* to represent persons or things respectively, both lead to new unities. The common element is either 'represented' or 'eliminated', depending upon its agreeability or disagreeability to repressive agency and to avoid common element in the constructed Image. Freud compares these elements as "determinatives" like those used in 'hieroglyphic script' which are not to be pronounced but serve merely to elucidate other signs. Freud goes on to develop concept of 'over determination'. Paul Ricouer has dealt at great length on this concepts of Identification and over determination in Freud as having Teleological and progressive (as opposed to regressive) elements in his philosophy without making it explicit that it is governed by 'law of representation' in Freud and as an inevitable and inexorable consequence of severe conditions imposed upon dream work. Ability of these determinatives to give birth to several Identifications and to condensation of an extraordinary amount of dream thoughts was discovered by Freud as a direct and crucial outcome of his acquaintance with contributions made by Darwinian scientist F. Galton.

Like above there are few more logical relations (not being considered here) represented by Dream Image and by which "Unconscious" is represented in Dream Image. Freud has described this process as, "in the process of interpreting dreams, we abandon reflection and allow involuntary ideas to emerge…….. As soon as we have done this, (getting rid off) unknown or, as we inaccurately say, 'unconscious' – purposive ideas take charge and therefore determine the course of involuntary ideas." (I.O.D.p.675).

Paul Ricouer has discussed its significance in larger context of Freud's 'Project' and subsequent works and influence on Freud by Helmoltz, Fechner and Von Hartman. Nevertheless **he has provided little attention to Galton and influence his discoveries exerted on Freud.** That is why possibly why Freud borrowed (Refer F & P.Ricouer); concept of 'ID' from Groddeck has not been explained satisfactorily. Nevertheless it is tentatively, correct to say that **to the discourse of unconscious Freud has assigned status of primitive language.**

It' status can be characterized by 'dialects' or 'hieroglyphics' at the same time (as Freud equates it with dialect). It is in Line with remarks by Paul Ricouer, "language itself works at the pictorial level". Without the help of such concept *(unconscious intentionality)* it is impossible to imagine 'who' marshals articulation of representations and expressions in dream image, 'who' evades, hoodwinks (the censorship) during Freud's 'self analysis' or 'who' works like Francis Galton, and is responsible for 'condensations'? Revolutionary Dream was a compromise structure, under repressive conditions exercised by resistance and the means at the disposal of 'ID', and expressed as a contest between the totally obliterated 'distant past' and 'recent image'.

Hence 'Self Analysis' was most protracted and painful process of training of the educationist himself, of ID, or ego- of bringing the unconscious, involuntary processes (unconscious intentions) of 'representations', which Freud ' observed' (discovery of his own "oedipal situation' after enormous struggle and practice) into its articulation as **self analysis.** Freud's, Relevance of this discovery can be discussed in relation to the dialectic intrinsic to condensation.

In above two sections, 'Re-writing or Reconstruction of History' & 'Psychoanalysis -The theory of Language' with their subsections I have devoted to one fundamental question, does I.O.D. offers us any method and means of interpretation, to re appropriate the social history, lost forever? I have attempted to show that Freud has been condemned forever for 'solipsistic' core of his theories (despite the insights appreciated by various quarters) has in fact swept it away by integrating all the three levels of imaginations, ***productive Imagination, associative imagination and phantasy level.***) by suitably retaining the basic bar between Pcs / Ucs. The correctness and suitability of the technique has been established by his treatment of Neurosis.

Representations in Typical Dreams and Neurosis

If we note that the object of investigation in Typical Dreams has not been Dream Image, alone but transformations and distortions the imagery undergoes, in the modes of representations, in view of impact of secular advance of repression in the emotional life of the mankind under new epoch of civilization, we realize why child's wishful 'Oedipus' phantasy remains suppressed – just in case of neurosis'. But 'Oedipus Complex 'is not 'Neurosis'. "Oedipus complex may justly be regarded as nucleus of Neurosis" (p. 380 Dev. Of libido). With Typical Dreams, and Oedipal Symbol Freud has introduced us to another Technique of Interpretation-Symbolic! Here Freud makes a transition to this technique of interpretation- to deal with symbolic elements of representation. He calls it as 'combined technique', " which on one hand rests on dreamer's associations and on the other hand fills the gaps from the interpreter's knowledge of symbols" (I.O.D. p. 470)

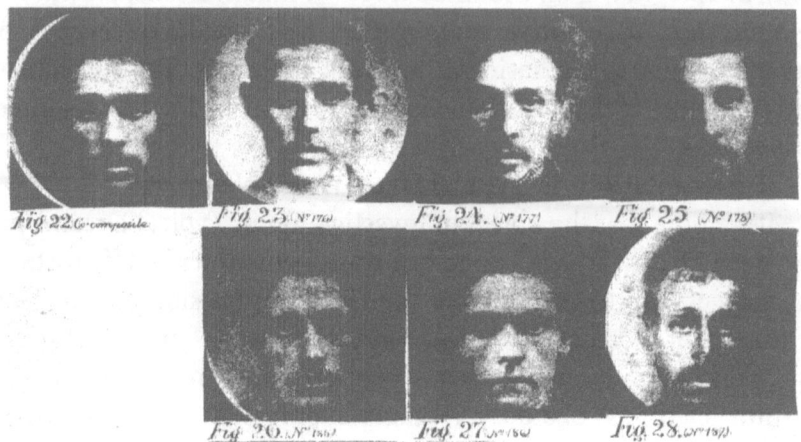

(- Winckelmann Vs Galton)

(e) Forgetting in Dreams and Trans-valuation.

In dealing with the scientific Literature on dreams Freud deals extensively on an important characteristics of dreams, namely why they are forgotten and the technique of recovering the 'lost portions of dreams'. He gives following causes for occurrence of this phenomenon.

- The dreams are forgotten because they fall to pieces after waking up.
- Dreams are forgotten because they hardly take over *ordered recollection* from waking life.
- After waking, moreover , the world of senses presses forward and at once take possession of the attention with a force which very few dreams can resist; in above summery Freud has captured and redefined the *aggressive nature of psychic repression* and at the same time shown the peculiar incompatible and upside down relationship between the conscious and unconscious. The portion of the 'dream thoughts' which suffers the most is preserved in dream image merely as transitory or an insignificant element or episode. Art of interpretation faces its toughest task in interpretation and *'revaluation'* of this portion of dreams. It has to work on the mutilated parts and doing so has to

exhaust the resistance offered to its significant value in the dream thoughts but entry of this element into dream.

This task is not easy. As a mandatory aspect of this technique Freud has accepted "as being just as important to interpret the smallest, least conspicuous and most uncertain constituents of the content of the dreams as those that are most clearly and certainly preserved'. This smallest, transitory detail finds its way into dream because 'it has some particular origin'. Freud could have identified such a phenomena *as one of the mechanisms of dream work, namely as part of distortion or displacement*. Instead Freud coined a different category to identify such indistinct piece of image, trans-valuation and a <u>distinct and marvelous 'source' of information</u> which enunciates relational aspect of such elements, between the dream thoughts and manifest dream.

Freud's analogy to describe their (of such elements) survival and existence in dream material as the 'fate' and 'state of things' of the survivors of group of people belonging to the earlier regime, after sweeping revolution in one of the republics of antiquity or the renaissance' is highly expressive. He says, "The noble and the powerful families which had previously dominated the scene were sent into exile and all the officers were filled by newcomers. Only the impoverished and powerless members of the vanquished families or their remote <u>dependent</u>s were allowed to remain in the city; and even so they did not enjoy full civic rights and were viewed with distrust".

Freud viewed this phenomena or process as historical or governed by a time trajectory. Freud says, "As we already know, however a *__complete transvaluation__* of all psychical vales takes place between the dream thoughts and the dream". This accounts for process of repression and thrust towards pushing the material into 'unconscious'.

As part of a method of presentation Freud discusses Forgetting in dreams at the beginning of the book and subsequently in the closing chapters of his book. What intervenes, between section of the book dealing with 'forgetting' and Chapter VII of the dream book are the chapters on *'logical relations' (disguised representation of logical relations) and 'considerations for representability'*. Reading of both these chapters allows us to understand that *distortion in dreams' is founded on this Tran valuation process*. Art of interpretation works against the resistance which is manifested during the course of discovering the '***withdrawal of its value***' from the manifest dream. Presence of such indistinct and floating elements confirms psychoanalytical dictum that it gives us a 'sure indication that we are dealing with a comparatively direct derivative of one of the proscribed dream thoughts". As a rule of research and investigation, in dreams logical relations represented are discovered. Freud says, "Never to attack the more intense elements of a dream but only the weak and indistinct ones".

It was one of the finest discoveries for Freud to realize that, "A direct derivative of what occupies a dominant position in dream thoughts can often only be discovered precisely in some transitory element of the dream which is quite *overshadowed* by the more powerful images". (p.443- IOD).***Trans-valuation thus is one of the most important mechanisms of distortion or disguise.*** It obliterates and hoodwinks the search and investigation and reveals resistance to its interpretation.

Psychoanalysis has taught us the significance of this discovery as a rule, applicable to events and identical phenomena in every day life or in human history as well. Latter on we will see that in E. P. Thompson's 'The Making..." the same concept of ***transvaluation in Dreams reappears as 'condescension' as same repressive force underlying forgetting is at work in human History as well..*** The value of the elements which occupies real dominant position in history or in dream thoughts is 'represented' by its 'derivative', transitory element due to powerful repression. A similar technique has been applied by Thompson to overcome distortions and disguising in history and look for sources of their appearance in periods of 'relaxations of repression'.

(f) Freud's 'Auxiliary Theories' Symbolism and Human Wok. – Derivations from Philology

At the end of the last sub-chapter, 'Representation of logical relations' and 'Forgetting in Dreams', I have focused on place of

'Oedipus Complex' in Freud's Interpretation of Dreams and its relation to 'self analysis'. .

.

In chapters, 'Dreaming and its functions' and 'Infantile Material' Freud has talked about *one more kind of Distortion*. Here the some of the latent dream thoughts are replaced by plastic images, concrete portrayals of the dream elements Large number of abstract thoughts are transformed into visual images as 'substitutes' of them in the manifest dreams. They are termed by 'plastic symbolism'. Schrener (1861- Freud calls him, discoverer of symbolism) had called it as 'dream-imagination', representing organisms, part of bodies or sexual acts. Now the role of 'symbolism' became 'central' since they defy the 'associative processes.

Freud developed a special 'technique of familiar picture puzzles' (p.152 Manifest and latent elements). However its status is not replacing the associative technique, "It forms a supplement to the latter and yields results which are only of use when introduced into it." (p.184, Symbols in Dreams) it. These are *substitutes, allusions,* of sexual objects. They are of *stereotypes sexual dream symbols*; nevertheless since they are 'Typical', representing, birth, death of close relatives like sisters, brothers, mother, nakedness, genitals etc. Their representations are vast, but interpretation of which yields monotonous results, nevertheless they impart total obscurity. Hence their importance. Treatment of these symbols and their interpretations, in dreams forced Freud to conclude that they are invariably sexual.

They represent unconscious thinking; hence they are the 'distortions' of other types. They represent the process of regression of dream thoughts to plastic images. It is my effort to demonstrate that for Freud they express and represent an acute tension between, *'the primitive history of the mankind' and the 'advent of commodity production'*.

To Freud's surprise and with his experience over years he realized that 'presence of symbols', posed highest difficulties in his technique of interpretation, then named as 'associative method' practiced by the patients. Freud discovered that the relations expressed by these symbols are not 'instituted by them during the process of dream formation'. ***Symbolization is readily found else where and is used in the dreaming process and is <u>not the result of dream work</u>. In such cases what produces these 'distortions?***

"We can learn about their presence in dreams from other and different sources, namely, fairy tales and myths (mythological parallels), legends, imaginative writings and dramatics, copious material, buffoonery and joke, from folk lore (from knowledge about popular manners, customs, sayings and songs). And from colloquial linguistic usages and poetics". Thus dream work does not take any part in the construction of Symbolic Relations' and are the prolonged result of pre- historical, work of transformation of human animal into human being as a result of a process of development of Culture.

Paul Ricouer remarks that Freud does not take note of this discovery. In his brilliant remark Ricouer "The confirmation of the sexual symbolism of dreams by the symbolism of myths is equivalent to a reduction of mythical to the oneiric – even though myths supply the element of speech in which ***semantics of symbolism*** has actually been built. (F & P. p.500) Concerns expressed by Paul Ricouer have been dealt below.

Freud's concerns were not different from those of Ricouer when he elaborated his theory of dream symbolism in the context of development of civilization particularly after the publication of first edition of I.O.D. and to assess the ramifications it can have. Confrontations with other disciplines and collections made by real professionals in anthropology, mythology, philology and folklore, brought out the richness and variations in symbolism in other fields, which are **not solely sexual symbols**. Freud puts forward the hypotheses that ***"symbols originally had a sexual significance latter acquired another applications and that further more toning down of representations by symbols into other kind of representations"***. This Freudian 'Auxiliary theories' originated from this hypotheses. Summery highlights are as follows.

1. Dream symbols are invariably sexual, representing human body, genitals, sexual acts etc. They are the stumbling blocs for interpretation since they are substitute visual images or objects distorted or displaced from their base.

2. A special supplementary technique was established for their interpretation and yields results only when introduced as part of associative technique. Little information can be provided by dreamer regarding their origin.

3. Number of times, they are monotonous and we can learn about their presence in dreams from other and different sources, discussed above. They are represented as parallels of dream symbols. In other fields, they are not solely sexual symbols. Freud puts forward the hypotheses that **"symbols originally had a sexual significance** latter acquired another applications and that further more toning down of representations by symbols into other kind of representations". The technique of interpretation of Dream Symbols (thing presentations) is derivative and function of these sources. Psychoanalytic practitioners can integrate them from other sources.

.4. In this sense, the invariably, sexual nature of dream symbols and subsequent variations of very rich types, prompted Freud to *construct a historical passage (from pre-history to history of civilization), hierarchy of symbolism*. The prehistoric modes of thoughts are thus preserved in dream symbols and their representations, as vestiges of processes which have gone into history. Secondly these expressions cross the language barriers. We do find variations in dream symbols, such as representing 'castration' and 'oedipal' symbols and variety of such Legends can be illustrated in histories of various nations and lands.

5. In observations made by Philologist Hans Sperber (Refer discussion above regarding 'Antithetical meanings...') Freud finds supportive hypotheses. 'Sexual needs have played the biggest part in the origin and development of speech. .... Further development of linguistic roots accompanied the *working activities of primal man*. ... In this sense sexual interest became attached to work. The primal man made work acceptable as were, by treating it as an equivalent of

and substitute for sexual activity. The words enunciated during work in common thus had two meanings. ... As time went on the words became detached from the sexual meanings and fixed to the work. In latter generations the Same thing happened with new words, which had a sexual *meaning and were applied to new forms of work. ...."* (p. 201-02 Intro. Lectures S. Freud). Hypotheses Freud has sketched further to understand reasons for presence of large number of sexual symbols, how dreams preserve earliest conditions (social) and symbolic relation (sexual and tools used in working activities etc.) as residue of verbal identity.

This has come under severe criticism from Ricouer for following reasons. 1) Freud does not draw any consequences from his own discovery regarding analogy between myths & dream symbols, "even though Freud is aware of that there is more in myths, fairy tales, sayings, and poetry than in dreams."(P.501 F & P) 2) Freud adopted this Non-Analytic Hypotheses to give dreams an advantage over myths. Ricouer underscores its value as linguistic. This hypotheses of ancient ambiguous roots, where in problem is solved by projecting it into 'basic language'. Here similarity cannot be justified as identity. 3) Earnest Jones intransigent defense of this Hypotheses by stressing the possibility that the sexual symbols can be the symbols of something else, since "sexual is always signified and not signifier" meaning that they can be the articulation of certain processes may be social or otherwise in nature used by dreams for expressions. 4) Freud may be mistaken in limiting the notion of symbols to 'stenographic signs', in which one discovers only, and nothing but the 'past' and not the dawn of meanings?

Ricouer finds it disconcerting and is extremely disturbed at this Hypothesis since it neither deals with the prospective symbols which can create and serve as the vehicles of new meanings nor represent creation of new meanings. .

g) Freud's 'Auxiliary Theories' – Symbols, Human Work & Popular Culture.

(From Interpretation of Dreams to Freud's mature theory of Human Civilization)

It is beyond the scope of this essay to treat this subject in detail. However as part of compulsion to understand place and role Freud assigned to symbolism in constitution of technique of interpretation I decided to deal with this subject and it's implications on historical context of his theory of neurosis. I felt that it is unjustified to say that Freud did not conceive hierarchy of symbols in a way Ricouer defines them as, a) symbols which are worn with use and no longer operative, b) symbols which are utilized in every day social life as nexus of social pacts and c) symbols with multiple significations and serving as vehicles of new meanings.

I differ with Paul Ricouer who characterizes Freud's hypotheses on symbols derived from Philology as disregarding creative moments. We can state here that the Dream symbolism hypotheses for Freud in psychic life signifies and represents an <u>internalization of historical process (rather a prehistoric process) of social sedimentation</u> and alienation with the advent of commodity production and as a consequence of sacrifice of instinctual satisfaction for the benefit of social order and first steps towards man's adulthood.

This is exactly the historical stage, the dawn of civilization Freud turned towards for a solution. 'Antithetical meanings of Primal words' merely presents the impending dialectic between linguistic articulation of sexuality and their <u>distorted expression as tools , weapons and activities through process of sublimation, affirmation and negation</u>. Freud could interpret dream symbols only through interpretation of *linguistic usages and prehistoric vestiges.* Dream thoughts become admissible in to consciousness only when expressed symbolically.

However Freud's discovery of these symbols themselves being instituted somewhere else, namely appropriated as remains of pre-civilization culture enables Freud to 'attack the whole problem (plethora of cultural expressions across the human civilization) from the direction of dreams". (p. 200 Symbols in dreams, Intro. Lectures).

By this he means interpretation of popular cultures an area and field for expansion of 'associative imagination for psychoanalysis'. This area however has been explored by Karl Mannheim and E.P. Thompson.

If this psychoanalytic discovery is carried through, for the benefit of and in the direction of various disciplines which Freud's encounters namely, Philology, Mythology, sociology, anthropology, folklore and other disciplines the 'Auxiliary Theory' will not remain "non-analytic Auxiliary theory". The reciprocity between the popular cultures in which birth of symbols appears and instituted / reappears as Dream Symbols *speaks well about the ability of psychoanalytic interpretative technique to grasp their meanings and thus contribute to venture in to interpretation of such cultures is well understood by Freud*. This is what he announces in his introduction to the third Edition (1911) of his Dream Book It only indicates the need for integration of psychoanalysis with other social-human sciences.

In fact within the so called 'identity between sexual and non sexual' Freud, knowingly or unknowingly has introduced the 'difference' and first element of 'process of distortion' and 'hiding'. This exactly has been ignored by Paul Ricouer while brushing aside the hypotheses. Freud sketches a historical and hypothetical process of subservience, subsumption and sublimation of sexual forces to new conditions of social development and work. This is probably the only reference in Freud where in Freud articulated theory of sublimation of forces of sexuality to conditions of human labor, **division of labor and labor itself becoming a general commodity with the passage of time.** Freud had very little idea what his discovery is going to lead to. In fact it can be stated that there are 'two' theories of symbolism in the hypotheses, first 'symbols' as the vestiges of past and second as 'distorted *(desexualized)* images' of human collective work!

In Preface to the third edition of IOD, he defines symbolism as 'unconscious thinking and ventures to "prophesy in what direction latter editions of the book will differ from the present one". "On one hand they will have closer contact with imaginative writings …. Will have to deal with …. The relation of dreams to neurosis and mental diseases". (Preface to third edition- 1911). Both these directions for Freud would pioneer the relationship between psychoanalysis and other human sciences.

For me Freud fail short of *defining this concept of 'distortion' identical to and as a direct precursor of commodity fetishism*. This concept does not conflict with Freudian archaic since both, deformation and repression are present. This also gives us an insight into close, integral link and relationship between 'two types of human alienation', in human social order. First one, downward, regressive the sexual or 'Oedipal' and second one resultant of 'civilization', caused by specific relation between 'capital and labor'. Their hierarchy or stratification of symbolism would be of interest to us.

If we take into consideration, latter Editions of IOD, Fifth edition (1918) and Preface to the third (Revised) English edition, we find only necessary alterations introduced in view of fresh discoveries on 'Neurosis'. The Introductory Lectures (1916-17), New Introductory Lectures (1933), and few other works have carried forward inclusion of these insights on relationship between Neurosis and dreams in the specific chapters devoted to dream analysis. His comment, 'but since then a profounder understanding of the neurosis has contributed towards the comprehension of dreams', demonstrate that he was more concerned with the new emerging social fabric which caused and led to a dangerous situations in human history, namely 'crisis of capitalism' in forties of last century..

His concerns became more inward with rise of war neurosis and fascism. He could analyze it as total break down *of relationship between sexuality* and human work, may lead to regression, crisis of sublimation implied in 'common neurotic state' of human kind. Crisis of civilization is founded on this regression. This had created for Freud need to explore in greater detail possible relationship of dreams to neurosis, phobias and other mental diseases. Freud clearly understood that he was dealing with human beings in the modern capitalist environment and "Motive of the civil society in the last resort is an economic one ...". Freud's formulations regarding the compulsion to work or exigencies of life of civil society to "divert the energies from sexual activity to work." (Intro. Lecture – Sexual Life of Human Beings) clearly expresses the antagonism and dialectical relationship between Sexual Instincts (Libido) and human work. Transformation *(sublimation) of sexual and other instinctual drives into 'economic' or more precisely into 'work drive'*

Freud's comparison of 'libido' and 'hunger' as fundamental drives is significant. What he could not realize is the importance of discovery and transformation of the instinctual drives into 'labor', 'activities' or 'work' lead to another set of <u>new **conditions in the world called 'advancing civilization'**</u>. The 'patricidal' drive itself is subjected to another set of conditions, in which large 'collectives', of working masses, with inherent capacity towards 'disclosures' and 'socialization' are born.

Carl Shorske's remarks "Dr. Freud left Thebes languishing still under the plague of politics" is clearly misplaced but at the same time, carry an element of truth. <u>With the Victorian background, S. Freud could not have been expected to possess the adequate technique to work on. This task and was left over to Historians like E.P. Thompson to explore.</u>

Despite above it is important that Freud has again and again expressed the fear of "Otherwise the instincts would break down every dam and wash away the laboriously erected work of civilization" (Intro. Lecture -) Freud encountered the expressions of such break down in Hysteria, Neurosis and variety of disorders. At latter stage war neurosis and subsequent the rise of Fascism supplemented his fears.

The dream symbols and images which were subjected to interpretation made him certain about the disjunction between the two. I have called this theory as 'Auxiliary Theory' which intends to demolish the last vestiges of Solipsism as rightly pointed out by Anthony Wielden... Freud's interpretation of dreams had a sharp focus on the fact that social institutes such as moral machinery, educational and production of wealth, were born in the wake of civilization harnessed, sheltered, tamed and sublimated the sexual-patricidal instincts in different forms.

I have attempted to differentiate Freud's articulation of two different kinds of 'distortions' in dreams. In one case it is close to what Paul Ricouer (like Benveniste) 'thing presentation' and other is close to 'word presentation'. Based on the mode of articulation Freud has already developed 'stratification of symbols', as stated above and which I will discuss little latter. Paul Ricouer identifies the first one as 'mechanism' bordering on supralinguistic 'when it mobilizes stereotyped symbols parallel to those ethnography finds in the great unities of meaning known as fables, legends". He continues in next passage- "On the other hand, displacement and condensation belong to the infralinguistic order------ One might say that dreams arise from a short-circuiting of the infra- and supralingusic. This jumbling of the infra- and the supralinguistc is perhaps the most notable language achievement of the Freudian unconscious (p. 405- F & P F- Paul Ricouer)".

To summarize, in spite of acceptance of validity of Paul Ricouer's appreciations and apprehensions that linguistic concepts of unconscious will open floodgates to equating it with ordinary language and undermining the basic conflict between Pcs/ Ucs would be disastrous, it should be noted that Freud treated symbolic articulations on different levels. In my view the symbolic articulations in dreams, representing 'working activities', 'tools' etc. can be termed as 'desexualized' (hiding the sexual connotations) and can be best be regarded as precursors to symbols we encounter in the *field of political economy and commodity-money-capital relationship*. In my view, Ricouer and Carl E. Schorske have missed out, few important elements of Freudian techniques of interpretation of symbols and his concerns in adopting this hypotheses (Auxiliary theories).

The Quest of the Modern Oedipus.

The Quest of Modern Oedipus.

(Dream is the mental product of antiquity and Neurosis is the mental product of emerging bourgeois mode of production)

Interpretation of Human Experience in Interpretation of dreams.

This section deals with 'demystification' or 'defetishization' of concept of Symbol, particularly 'symbol par excellence' 'Oedipus'. I am talking about 'chapter' Typical Dreams which has a special well planned and thought out place in Freud's presentation of his treaties on dreams interpretation. The theme ties Sigmund Freud and Karl Marx in the areas of methodology. Freud has refrained himself from detailed discussion on hysteria & neurosis till he gets down to 'Typical Dream'. These dreams are not those of S. Freud but are dreams, "which everyone has dreamt alike and which we are accustomed to assume must have the same meaning for every one" .It is followed by discussions under ' considerations of representatbility', and 'representation by symbols and in greater depth under chapter VII of the book.

Typical dreams have following additional characteristics

a) They are the dreams 'dreamt by every one and make use of 'common expressions', symbolic fragments' by utilizing them from sources which are not the result of the dream work.

b) Dreamer fails 'as a rule to produce the associations', in fact they become obscure. They exhibit abundance of symbols in the dream text.

c) They are the seat of the 'childhood', 'primal' and 'prehistoric' suppressed desires and impulses. The suppressed and forbidden wishes break through in the dreams by finding shelter into 'unobjectionable' desires capable of entering into the 'consciousnesses.

d) They are well 'qualified to throw light on sources of dreams, because they 'presumably arise from same source in every case.

This chapter is marked by discussion on "Oedipus Complex' and revolves around the stories of "Oedipus Rex' and Shakespeare's 'Hamlet' which Freud feels that both have grown on the same soil and both are response of Imaginations of creative poets to 'infantile material', found in these Typical dreams' which manifest child's relationship with his parents.

Carl Schorske has called this chapter as central, since Freud could push his IOD as a whole from personal <u>infantile experience 'to the childhood of the human race'</u>. Chapter Typical dreams' has been characterized by him as the deepest mythical layer, where the 'individual experience of the unconscious' is found embedded in the universal <u>archetypal experience of the primitive man.</u> It is difficult to accept Carl Schorske's identification of 'Typical Dreams' as 'mythical layer'. *Freud discusses this chapter not so much as 'mythical level' but as first detailed discussion about fundamental relationship between dream life and waking life and as dream image and hysterical or neurotic symptoms under advancing stage of Civilization.* .

Clearly Carl Schorske has attempted to differentiate Freudian endeavor from that of Oedipus Rex and has instead identified Freud with 'Hamlet' where Freud's quest for truth ended up in achieving 'personal salvation by overcoming his Rome neurosis' and by keeping the entire Austro- German socio polity languishing under the threat of sweeping Anti Semitism, which finally ended up with social neurosis and triumph of Fascism.

Here my attempt is to treat IOD initially as scientific treaty and subsequently as personal tragedy and but co-relate them after summarizing Freud's achievements, by focusing on his methodology and treating his 'personal experience' as subservient to it.

I have stated earlier that Freud's <u>method of investigation and presentation</u> where in dream has been treated as <u>'a cell form'</u>, now calls for, interpretation of neurosis as a complex phenomena, as transition or transformation of dream into neurosis, Hysteria, phobias etc., the complex forms, in a way Karl Marx. Treated transformation of commodity form into money form and further into capital form. This is the result of the <u>additional determinations</u> and social laws introduced by historical process, of dawn of civilization and advancement of 'repression in the emotional life of the mankind'. The antithetic of sexuality and human work introduces this symbolism as a 'distortion and a veil' which appears in and through dreams, and marks the separation of two epochs.

As against Carl Schorske's treatment, Paul Ricouer has commented that despite modifications in latter Editions Freud left the interpretation of Oedipus Myth to the sub section of Typical Dreams containing death wishes, and more particularly child's death wish against his parents.

Paul Ricouer has treated interpretation of 'Oedipus Rex' and 'Hamlet' as applied psychoanalysis for interpretation of culture by way of analogy. ---

On the other hand, for S. Freud <u>it was a multifold exercise and Freud approaches the question of Oedipus</u> by mediating through the invaluable, extensive and rich psychoanalytic experience he gained in the course of psychoanalytic treatments (and is not based on his 'self analysis' alone) regarding what forms the foundations of 'psychical impulses' and which determines the 'symptoms of the latter neurosis'.

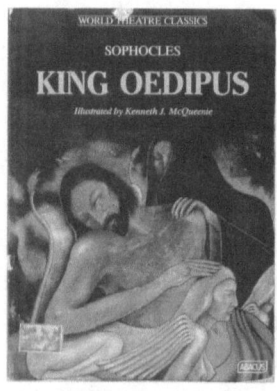  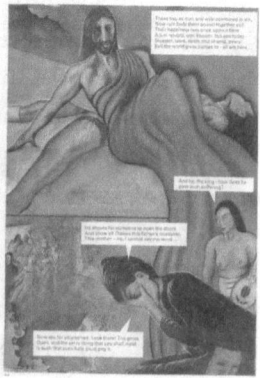

-Oedipus Tragedy.

I have divided this segment into four parts.
- Socio Epochal Setting of Oedipus.
- Freud's treatment of Oedipus in Typical Dreams.
- Carl Schorske's Patricide in IOD
- Impact of Interpretation of Dreams on S. Freud's latter theories.

Socio Epochal setting of 'Oedipus'.

The universal validity of Freud's 'hypotheses' and 'experience' has been compared with the Oedipus legend from antiquity having 'profound and universal power' to move the audience and the reader. This comparison has been stressed by Freud himself so as to amplify the 'resonance between 'the work of psychoanalysis', and "Oedipus Rex". The storey of Oedipus is nothing other than, painful process evolving with cunning delays and ever mounting excitation' is 'psychoanalytic' and 'self analytic' human experience. So both are mediated by 'human experience'. The experience which stretches out from the epoch of 'primal history' to emerging civilization. This chapter integrates the universal –general observations, experiences of his patients and his own personal experience as Schorske has rightly stated.

As scientific treaty, as 'self analysis' and as 'experience' of common man', the battles are fought on the arena of 'socio-cultural' plane. It was the spiritual gain of psychoanalysis as science to achieve something beyond 'Art and pleasure principle'. A 'hope for the future' for setting up of humanly comprehensible social life for the patients. I have stressed that for Freud this would not have been possible without inherent ability of psychoanalysis to transcend solipsism and comprehend universal experience.

The code of conduct, of prohibition of incest was institutionalized as social, cultural and psychical morality at the dawn of civilization. They have been banished and repressed forever. The repressed instincts are always on alert to exert themselves, express themselves in and through dreams, neurosis, hysterical phobias, obsessions; delusions and symptoms are the expressions of the struggle against the formidable forces of repression. They become issues of urgent social concern.

To sum up Freud's approach to Epochal Setting of Oedipus-Dreams are product of sleep but others are those of waking life. But in the face of week ego it is very difficult to provide 'representations' to these instincts in dreams and other mental products. Beneath every hysterical or neurotic symptom psychoanalyst finds presence of sexual symbol, which finds 'hiding place' behind what appears to be 'inconspicuous'. These veils are provided by superstitions, customs, social myths, linguistic sayings and proverbs.

Work of psychoanalysis and interpretation is inverse of or reversal of 'dream work', of disguise, of compression, of condensation, of condescension, of censorship, of displacement and that of regression. This interpretative process and technique of handling resistances are simultaneously at work as part of psychoanalytic practice. In psychoanalytic process, which passes through patient's resistance, rejection, defense and transference, both the processes are at work, in a manner of a protracted struggle. Patient has to spend enormous energy in unveiling the repression which puts a virtual bar on the expression of ideas, specifically the infantile-primal desires. On the other hand   psychoanalyst has to possess a diligent craftsmanship in handling this resistances and transferences.

Thus double edged process, compounding of two discourses, discourse of meaning and discourse of energy, the first one is subservient to discourse of energy and force. When both stand in dialectical relationships with each other, they become complimentary to each other, interpretative process finally guarantees the success of psychoanalysis.

It is a process of 'temporary suspension of 'conscious' in order to gain access into the 'unknown', namely the 'unconscious'. For unconscious to become conscious it has to transgress or cross the barrier insulating the unconscious. Since as we have seen conscious has three modes of existence, 'unconscious (UCS), preconscious (PCS) and conscious (CS), process of gaining access to unconscious desires and instincts is also energy overcoming process.

Unconscious is the seat of 'incestuous' desires' and are steadfastly prevented from becoming conscious, not only by 'primary repression' but equally by secondary repression also. Psychoanalysis not only assigns topographical places for them but also chronological-historical locations with different and exclusive laws of their expressions in psyche and in culture.----

Hence in historical terms, Shakespeare's 'Hamlet' should have formed the most appropriate form of Freud's subject of enquiry in 'Typical Dreams. However methodologically it would have been <u>incorrect and hence unacceptable</u> to solve the mystery of this 'complex cultural product'. The solution to this mystery was provided by 'Oedipus Rex' and it supplied him the clues to the understanding not only the cultural expression of universal 'Typical dreams' but also the Character <u>of 'Hamlet'</u>!

Freud has articulated the same framework in matured theoretical formulation, when he says, "in spite of all the latter development that occurs in the Adult, none of the mental Formations perish. All the wishes, Instinctual impulses, modes of reactions and attitudes of childhood are still demonstrably present in the maturity and at appropriate circumstances can emerge once more. They are not destroyed but are overlaid -to use the spatial mode of description which psychoanalytic psychology has been obliged to adapt. Thus it is part of the nature of the mental past that, unlike the Historic past it is not absorbed by its derivatives, it persists (Whether actually or only potentially) alongside what has proceeded from it."(Claims of Psychoanalysis --p.49.).

To paraphrase Paul Ricouer, the 'Oedipus situation' thus sets up a conflict between Civilization and mighty instincts, unguided by a weak 'id' and 'ego'. Historically, psychic and social repression is constituted by ossification and sedimentation of moral and legal institutions. So far political – radical historical sciences have been dealing with authoritative repressive powers of legal, political, social and economic institutions. (Bourgeoisie mode of production and reproduction and Fetishism thereof). Freud draws parallel with powers exercised by psychical censorship which makes wish fulfillment of dream unrecognizable. This is identified as dream distortion (p. 223 IOD). Freud is not limiting his analysis to the constitution of 'Oedipus Complex' as a result of primary repression but how in fact it gets firmly entrenched due to 'overlying of the secondary repression' and how their expressions can emerge "at appropriate circumstances more".

This process is also accompanied by what Freud calls the 'dissolution of Oedipus complex and identification with parental agency or authority and which results into strengthening of Oedipus complex. Hence the 'phantasy aspect of '<u>Oedipus Complex'</u> is <u>subsumed by real 'phantasy'</u> Hence <u>Dreams exhibiting death</u> <u>wishes are common for 'normal' people and their Dreams and do</u> <u>not constitute 'abnormality'. On the other hand Neurosis, Hysteric</u> <u>symptoms, phobias and other complex products of waking life.</u> <u>They are far more 'concrete' expressions and indicative of</u> enormous proliferation of this conflict between the repressive force and the Oedipal desires. I feel Schorske has misunderstood the difference in these two products of mental life when 'psychoanalyzing' Freud for his Neurosis.

Freud subordinates all cultural aspects of 'Oedipus' to his scientific treaty on typical dreams and <u>restricts treatment of Oedipus Rex and</u> <u>Hamlet to his analytical and therapeutic procedure and technique,</u> <u>i.e. purely as part of his scientific treaty</u>.

<u>Freud's treatment of Oedipus in Typical Dreams.</u>
(Dreams and hysterical symptoms)

Oedipus the son of Laius, the King of Thebes, and Jacosta was exposed as infant because

an Oracle had warned Laius that the still born child would be his father's murderer. The unfolding of this story takes a biting turn with break out of plague and with messenger's reply that the plague will cease only when the murder of Lauis is driven out from the land.

The whole drama and action of play, is this process of enquiry for identification of the murderer and revelation that Oedipus himself is the unwitting, 'unconscious' murderer of his father and took his mother as his wife. Horrified by this disclosure, a process undertaken by Oedipus himself, and which passes through unbearable excitement and horror, Oedipus blinds himself and forsakes his home. 'The Oracle is thus fulfilled'. Freud likens this with the 'work' of psychoanalysis.

Let us see how Freud distinguishes significance of Psychoanalytic discourse for the psychoanalyst and for patie(analizand).

This psychoanalytic work involves and includes, both, method of investigation of a phenomena and technique like a therapeutic procedure and method of interpretation of meanings through meanings. From the outset and from the point of view of an analyst , from beginning to an end it is 'work' and which works on 'work' of the analyzand , For patient, it is the 'work' of <u>carrying out his own analysis.</u> <u>This third work involves, 'what he was 'unconscious' of, a process of</u> <u>self discovery and involving horror crossing the boundaries of this</u> <u>'separating Bar'. and Discovery of once own 'infantile desires (of</u> <u>death wish against father' and 'lust for mother'.) For psychoanalyst,</u> <u>more importantly it's a discovery of the 'mechanisms of repression, of</u> <u>entering into area named 'un-knowable, where the patient discovers</u> <u>the presence of these wishes'. Thus for psychoanalyst experience and</u> <u>'mechanisms of Dreams' and 'Neurosis' are disclosed, brought to</u> <u>light</u>...

Sigmund Freud in the style of Moses the Law-giver

Freud's Contribution to Dreams and Art
the Frozen Moment
Illustration of Composite Image
Cinematic Movements – in Analysis of
Sequence of Emotions, thought processes and
Postures in Sculpture- Moses of Michelangelo

- Freud –The Modern Oedipus in the style of Moses.

But why this differentiation of 'Dream Mechanisms and Mechanisms of Neurosis'? In Chapter typical dreams, Individual dreams appear only as its part of typical dreams. Hence *existence of Oedipus complex is Typical*, i.e. on one hand it appears as a social myth and on the other hand appears as Symbol residing in each of us *and* has two fold existences. The answer lies in differential treatment given to two different works of Art and culture. Oedipus Rex and Hamlet have come under Freud's scrutiny not so much as works of Art but as, 'self analysis' and *as validation of his scientific treaties on interpretation of Typical Dreams and first step* towards theory of neurosis.

Jack J. Spector in his 'The Aesthetics of Freud' regards Freud's treatments of Oedipus and Hamlet as his own obsessive identification with them as vehicles of self expressions. However his identification with Moses of Michelangelo is ambivalent.. His secular identification with Egyptian father figure enabled him to castigate his Jewish cultural heritage. As 'law giver' Freud controlled his rage against his erstwhile co-worker Jung and his Swiss Followers. He emulated Moses also out of anxiety to loose into the 'mob' of his sons, "upon whom his eye is turned-the mob which can hold fast no conviction...." (Freud- Moses---) It is clear that he could never overcome obsession of Father –Son, Master-Slave relations. Similar was his relationship with Goethe. Beyond childhood recollection Freud disliked psychoanalyzing Goethe as it was with Moses. Hence we must conclude that he did not have similar identifications with Oedipus and Hamlet.

The difference in the 'making of these two great creative works of Art'. Reference to Jocasta's consolation of Oedipus (Jacosta refers to dreams many people dream) in the drama, gives Freud the clues to the origin of this drama. 'The storey of Oedipus is the reaction of the imagination to these typical dreams'. In case of Oedipus Rex' the child's <u>wishful phantasy</u> that underlies is ***brought into the open and realized as in the dream***. In Hamlet, it ***remains- repressed***; and just as in case of Neurosis, - we learn about <u>its existence</u> from the inhibiting consequences'. The 'changed treatment' of the same material 'reveals the whole difference in the mental life of two widely separated epochs of civilization.'

The heart of the Oedipus storey centers on quest for truth. Compulsion towards 'investigation is 'from without' i.e. from outside, overcoming the social crisis and disaster caused by plague. His investigation involves agonizing, painful experience marked with excitement. The anger followed by ardent pursuance of truth which springs and proceeds from 'mystery of birth' and passes through protracted passage of curiosity, resistance, distress, break up and shattering of pride and ultimately enlightening -painful wisdom. Drama involving realization of 'Oedipal situation' and disclosure through intellectual –emotional exercise in order to resolve the dark enigma. The outcome of the exercise is 'spiritual' in which Oedipus emerges as Champion and star but tragically ends up by sinking into "seas of anguish, whelmed beneath a raging tide –"The experience in tragedy of truth is determined by the material of dreams". Paul Ricouer has vigorously elaborated on Freud's concept of over determination of symbol as in works of Arts and not as part of scientific treaty.

In the shortest, sweeping and brilliant analysis of "Hamlet" the Epochal creation of Shakespeare", Freud has traced back Hamlet's inhibition in fulfilling the task set for him by his "father's Ghost"to take vengeance on the man who did away with his father and married his mother. In order to grasp the inner motives underneath the 'strange inaction' of Hamlet, Freud, skillfully exercises his technique of interpretation, to dig into his stirrings of childhood desires and impulses in the mind of the Poet Author of Hamlet'!

Freud says, "Hamlet is able to do anything -- except take vengeance on the man who did away with his father and took that father's place with his mother, the man who shows him the repressed wishes of his own childhood as realized.". "Here I have translated into conscious terms, what was bound to remain <u>unconscious in Hamlet's mind</u>."(I. O.D. Typical Dreams.)

Freud was aware that he was presenting and throwing light on the 'so called' inexplicable behavior of Hamlet in the context of the emerging modern civilization or bourgeois social mode of production and reproduction. However Freud had to turn towards Sophocles's 'Oedipus Rex' to present it's similarity with psychoanalytical situation. Human experience involved in Psychoanalytic situation was discovered to have a complete resonance with 'Oedipus Rex' and could bring the ***human experience at the centre stage of the scientific treaty 'Interpretation of dreams'. Thus experience and hypotheses become one integrated.***

Paul Ricouer's treatment of this 'singular experience' is radically different. He sees Hamlet as extension of 'Oedipus Rex'. Freud's analysis of "the Hysteric Hamlet", who hesitates to kill mother's lover, it is because within himself lies "the obscure memory that he himself had mediated the same deed against his father because of his passion for his mother" (F & P. p.191 Paul Ricouer). Appreciating Freud's treatment of Oedipus and Hamlet relationship, Paul Ricouer remarks, "*If Oedipus reveals the aspect of destiny, Hamlet reveals the guilt attached to the complex".* He asks, 'What makes the individual secret universal and ethical- if not the involvement in the institutions"? Ricouer puts it brilliantly, 'Oedipus complex is <u>incest dreamt</u>'. The internalization of the primal desires and their persistence in spite of enormous advancement of civilization and in spite of it's 'anti- social character' and progressive renunciation, it has remained the ***most terrifying concern for Freud...***

In Typical Dreams, Oedipal Complex and Symbol forms the 'Nucleus' and which has been shown to influence the psychic course of law governing condensation, that is to ***provide the regressive path for Collapse or condensation of Present towards the Archaic Past. This law inexorably works with force to override the barriers posed by Human Development through work and Labor of centuries of civilization. In Typical Dreams S. Freud differentiates this 'influence' under different historical circumstances. Here we are again reminded by Freud's remarks, But 'Oedipus Complex 'is not 'Neurosis'. "Oedipus complex may justly be regarded as nucleus of Neurosis" (p. 380 Dev. Of libido).***

As an attempt to introduce the differentiation of Dreams and Neurosis and to highlight the further complications faced by Psychoanalytic treatment, Freud confronts two great tragedies, "Oedipus Rex' and 'Hamlet". For S. Freud at the foundation of both these plays is the 'Oedipal situation' or oedipal drama, expressed in 'Typical Dreams'. Outlined characteristics are as follows.

In case of Hamlet, the people (audience) have remained completely in dark regarding the character of the hero. In case of Oedipus Rex' his destiny moves us, only because it might have been ours". This is since, 'There must be something which <u>makes voice within us ready to recognize the compelling force</u> of destiny".

Thus the storey which 'resolves' the 'dark enigma' to end the looming threat of plague, the drama of truth, has been built on <u>three layers</u> with **<u>overdetermind ending</u>**, in which influence of Oedipus' is 'overwhelming' and manifesting at each stage.

A) 'The secret of birth and the curiosity built around it',
b) 'the enormous anger towards sear and resistance to disclosure, and

c) 'self recognition amidst crumbling of pride and search for light'.

One flows out of the preceding, from the sphere of 'libido' to sphere of 'self consciousnesses. At the same time what proceeds as next stage derives it's meanings from the earlier stage of drama. However like 'psychoanalyst' the force of truth is derived from the sear, while patient's initial stage resembles the dark side of the Sphinx. The second stage involves the unleashing of the anger towards the truth and attempt to exonerate oneself. The third stage has a passage through breakdown of pride of the king Oedipus and 'self knowledge'. The treatment of Oedipus and interpretation of symbol involves disclosure or defetishization of mystery and revival of history of master and slave.

Contrast between two poetic works, can now be highlighted.

In ' Oedipus" the child's wishful phantasy is brought into open and realized, while in case of Hamlet' it remains suppressed and – just as in case of neurosis we only learn of it's existence from it's inhibiting consequences'.

While the poet (Sophacles) unravels the past, brings to light the guilt of Oedipus, he is at the same time compelling us to recognize our own minds, in which those same impulses though suppressed are still to be found"...

In Oedipus Rex 'while the poet unravels the past', brings to light the guilt of Oedipus, and <u>complete revelation carried throug</u>h by the Hero, the 'people have remained completely in dark as to the character of the Hero' in case of Hamlet, who is able to do anything except take vengeance on the man who did away with his father and took his father's place and showed him the suppressed wishes of his childhood realized Freud says, he has 'translated into conscious terms, what was <u>bound to remain</u> unconscious in Hamlet's mind.' Beneath the Hysteria' exhibited by Hamlet, Freud says ***<u>poet's own mind which confronts us in Hamlet</u>"*** (p. 368 IOD- S. Freud). The conflict which manifested in the 'distaste of 'sexuality' expressed by Hamlet, took possession of the poet's mind more and more reached it's extreme expression in 'Timon of Athens'. Freud concludes that 'it can only be the poet's mind which confronts in Hamlet', Freud scans through Shakespeare's biography and like interpretation of dreams,

Freud 'over interprets' the neurotic symptom to grasp the deepest layer of the impulses in the mind of the creative writer'

The characteristic differences only highlight what Freud says, that the process of revealing in the play (Oedipus Rex) can be 'likened' with that of psychoanalysis but not 'identical'. What intervenes between them is the further complex product of mind, 'neurosis'. Oedipus Rex is the creation at the dawn of civilization; Hamlet is the product within the milieu of advancing civilization which has made the 'secular advance of repression in the emotional mind of the mankind'. Thus Hamlet' mediates between Oedipus Rex and Psychoanalysis. The mighty secondary repression transforms the response of the imagination to dream material into neurosis.

In Hamlet the *'Hysteric Symptom' of 'not able to take action against the person 'who did away with his father'* is treated as 'satisfaction of a revived wish dating back to childhood' is based on Freud's own experience with his patients and 'with himself'. We can recall Freud's two discoveries beneath such behavior. *'Thinking and experiencing were the same thing had a reference to the hysterical symptom' and symbol of male urinal belonged to the same connection"* (P. 310- Freud's Revolutionary Dream)). The hidden rebellious content of the dream or hysteric symbolization was discovered by Freud in interpretation of his own 'Revolutionary Dream'.

It is noteworthy that Freud discovered his *own hysterical symptom* in the final episode of dream of 'helping to urinate' his father. "And indeed the whole rebellious content of the dream, with its *lese majesti'e* and its derision of the higher authorities, **went back to rebellion against father** of his country, the father is the oldest, first, and for children the only authority, and from his autocratic power the other social authorities have developed in the course of the history of human civilization" (P. 310 IOD Freud). The derision was expressed in construction of what appears to be rare and precious object out of trivial and preferably comic worthless material, unconsciously created by Hysterical subjects in their waking life.

However there is no justification for Carl Schorske's comparison of discovery of Hysterical symptom in Freud's dream with that of Hamlet for the reason that unlike the latter, the former is not a 'social expression' nor the 'Oedipus Desires' have been represented by means of 'Identification' with singular person- in terms of names, physical characteristics, gestures, transference of psychical intensities etc. have taken place and which are hallmarks of 'Neurosis and Hysteria' of waking life. There is no process involved by which emotions and desires originally associated with one person, such as a parent or sibling, are unconsciously shifted to another person or substituted like in case of Hysterical Phobias. *Identification underlies beneath the phenomena where "Thinking and experiencing were the same thing had a reference to the hysterical symptom" In short 'symptom' cannot be equated with phenomena just as Freud says; Oedipus Complex is nucleus of Neurosis and not neurosis.*

Freud's important objective in 'Typical Dreams' was to present human experience in two different epochs of civilization. On the other hand as part of 'self analysis' it could be said that Freud found universal experience in details of his singular experience.

Construction of Dreams and Day Dream

e dreams, they are wish-fulfillments; dreams, they are based to a great ent on impressions of infantile ierience; like dreams, they benefit by a tain degree of relaxation of isorship...

They stand in much the same relatio to the childhood memories from whic they are derived as do some of the baroque palaces o Rome to the ancient ruins whose pavements and columns have provided the material for the more recent structures.

- Construction of Dreams

Carl Schorske's Patricide in IOD

For Paul Ricouer and Carl Schorske both have grasped that Freud's discovery of 'Oedipal desires' as decisive and focused in 'singular infantile experience' in the course of his 'self analysis' but they differ on significance of that experience. Paul Ricouer concludes that its universality was 'seen in the details of singular experience', on the other hand for Carl Schorske, Freudian experience was *'individualized'*.

Carl Schorske sees Freud's Oedipus' as not of Rex <u>but that of a thinker searching for his own identity</u>. By clinical understanding of the etiology of his own Neurosis, unlike another Jewish German politician, Edward Laskar Lassale (who failed in duel, with his opponent over a woman), Freud <u>could conquer his own sexual temptations (For his mother)</u>, Freud could demonstrate that 'Sex is stronger than politics, the dream (Freud's dream 'Autodidasker) seems to say, but science can control the sex' (p 201, P & P in Freud's IOD.). *Let me summarize Schorske's arguments which run as follows.*

1) In face of and troubled by rising tide of 'anti Semitism' in Austrian socio political situation, Freud's 'repressed instinctual impulses' like Juno's threat had subversive implications and warning to those in political authority. Freud's attempt in latter pages of IOD seems to be dispelling or assuaging the fears his sweeping findings can arouse. Like Shakespeare's Hamlet, Freud identified his political obligations and impulses with those of his father, explaining them away as attributes of his father's ghost, decided to bend before the Austrian rational polity.

2) In the Phantasy of Recognition for 'Interpretation of Dreams' by two thirds majority in Austrian Parliament". Carl Shorske Quotes Freud in his criticism. It at once becomes (and Freud was certainly conscious of) clear from Freud's quote that a 'Creative writer and a day dreamer were playing with his infantile Phantasy and childhood ambition. ---

Any one who is familiar with I.O.D. can easily recognize its construction and origins. The motive force of every phantasy is unsatisfied wish. Like every phatasy it 'strings together' three moments in the life of creative writer like S. Freud. The occasion which provoked the phantasy, his promotion to the position of Assistant Professor in face of growing anti –Semitism (fascisization) in Austrian socio-political life, the childhood ambition 'to come to something' and the 'infantile' 'Oedipal desire' are compressed and the emotions invested in these moments are cathected into a 'playful' imagined object reality as 'recognition of Psychoanalysis as Human science' by two thirds majority. Psychoanalysis assumes the ***role of 'Oedipus Rex' of the Modern Epoch*** who resolved the dark enigma and warns the humanity of danger of 'return of the repressed'. This Phantasy created was meant to overpower the growing uncomfortable and despairing situation of the Austrian Polity and we should call it a "child's play".

3) Schorske's analysis of tragic compromise of modern Oedipus-S. Freud with Austrian Authorities concludes that, Freud the "unreddler of the riddles, who found the key to the human condition in the story of Oedipus was also a lover of jokes". His mere fantasy of being recognized by the Austrian Parliament, was fulfillment of his dream desire to be 'recognized' accepted the title of 'Professorship' and celebrated his promotion as professional in the caricature of a political triumph"! Freud the 'Modern Oedipus' opted for kneeling before the Minerva's ruined temple to overcome his Rome Neurosis".

Carl Schorske who quotes Freud's letter to Wihelm Fliess, Freud's reflections on, "to break with my strict scruples" after he had completed *Interpretation of Dreams*. Freud himself "confesses for cultivating the powerful. …. Freud found his success tainted by guilt." In Freud's own words, "I have learnt that the old world is governed by Authority, just as the new is governed by Dollar. I have made my first bow to authority". (P. 183- Patricide in Freud).

This was the tragic end of Modern Oedipus, Professor Sigmund Freud, <u>who bowed before the authority and before the Austrian socio-political reality, as scientist and as Jew, as citizen and son.</u> Hence as Carl Schorske says, about the deepest layer of Interpretation of dreams, Freud gave this struggle, both outer and inner, its fullest, most personal statement and his great struggle for recognition ended up with temporary truce and compromise with liberalism. Unfortunately the compromise also could not last and prevent the woes of psychoanalysis from Fascist onslaught. Freud's uncompromising attitude with forces of fascism only vindicated Freud's commitments for truth and elements of validity of his theory of Civilization and its crisis.

It is regrettable that Freud, as Jew, never could have come to terms with Karl Marx's conclusions on 'The Jewish Question, "The social emancipation of the Jew is the emancipation of society from Judaism'.

Impact of Interpretation of Dreams on S. Freud's latter theories

As I have stated above, with discovery of social character of sexual forces in their manifestation', and discovery of Dream symbols having born during the dawn of popular culture and their universal character, *Freud pronounced the end of psychical solipsism.*

The universal conditioning of psychical life is further amplified in Freud's latter writings

in the various statements, "We believe that civilization is to a large extent being constantly created anew, since each individual who makes a fresh entry into human society repeats this sacrifice of instinctual instinctual Satisfaction for the benefit of the whole community." (S. Freud- 'Introduction to ...').

In Freud's scientific endeavor and with it's method, and 'self analysis', Freud devised 'an epoch making interpretation of Human experience in Which everyday life, social, political events and practice can be shown to be epiphenomenal expression or influence of or determined by Repressed psychical forces i.e. 'Oedipus Complex'. In his personal statement he also reconstructed history of his life long struggle with Austrian Socio-political reality as a scientist, as citizen and as a son. This forms his first experience. Another experience was psychoanalytic experience. Here in both ways, Carl Schorske's comparison of Freud with St. Augustine's Confessions ceases.---

His concern was the rising tide of anti-Semitism and at latter stage war neurosis, in which he saw Threat to civilization arising out of revival and return of original aims of instinctual forces and their destructive dimensions.

Carl E. Schorske discovered only the weak flank in Freud's efforts. However, the most important characteristics Freud noted about *crisis under modern Civilization are spurned due to 'Detachments*

of social forces of sexuality from sublimation through human work'. By focusing on the differences between dream and neurosis, Oedipus rex and Hamlet, Freud encounters challenges which are much stiffer and daunting than faced by **Sophocles Oedipus**. It is the secondary repression, which further strengthens the primary repression and arrests the efforts of creative Art, from carrying forward accomplishing of task of disclosure, it results into Neurosis or Hysteria. The task falls on the shoulders of Science of Psychoanalysis, Plague or world war, catastrophic crisis or 'anti Semitism', the ignorance or neurosis has to be defeated from <u>within or overcome the challenges which are far greater in magnitude and complexity than those of Oedipus.</u>

The Science he founded, in Paul Ricouer's words, 'Psychoanalysis a diligent exercise and practice'. This search involves risking of life, its existence, prestige and pride, of everything which is at stake and which chains human being to the social order of relationships. This I call as the second experience. This entirely stems from and welded by practice of technique developed in the course of treatment.

In spite of epoch making achievements, Psychoanalysis could not **explore adequately his 'Auxiliary Theory' he intended to expound.** The Dream symbols express the last vestiges, nevertheless the 'mediations 'between popular cultures and psychic life of social individuals. Psychoanalysis as science which exploded the solipsism from 'within' of individual psyche' remained 'unequipped' to address to the social Neurosis and to popular culture of working masses. *This is the area which in my opinion provided passage for E.P. Thompson's studies and thus as continuation of Freudian ventures*.

<u>Freud, the Modern Oedipus, in his self analysis, represented efforts and hope of mass of common people struggling against Neuro</u>sis, however left over the unfinished task of integrating his theories of imagination, historical laws of representations of images and of human experience for renewed scientific exploration. Freud who warned those at the helm of the power, and 'pictured the subversive threats of the instincts, in a mocking jest, found his struggle for recognition ending in a wish fulfilled in his promotion as Associate Professor.

It appears that Freud sustained this phantasy through to the end of his life which retained his faith in Liberal democracy. Psychoanalysis addressed itself to Humanity for conquest of the repressed, to control the 'storm unleashed by sexual instincts' and aimed at becoming the Science of common man finally became victim of Fascism and War Neurosis at the end of his life. ***Quest of Oedipus thus ended in another tragedy.***

Symbols and Historical Trajectory!

Historically, repression is accompanied by universalization of commodity production under Capitalism, by diversion of sexual aims and their redirection to higher social aims with the aim of taming the sexual instincts. His discovery of dream symbols as born amidst the dawn of the popular culture and their role as mediators between dream life and waking life should be regarded as one of the profound insights for historians.

For Biologists, Freud's concept of Civilization had Lamarckian traits. His formulations such as, "The mental past persists along side with what has proceeded from it" indicates that his it's a profound integration of Evolutionary theory with Lamarkianism.

Castration complex or Oedipus complex forms the permanently subsumed psychical state within what historically developed form of Civilization. We have seen above Freud's Auxiliary Theory based on findings by Philologist Hans Sperber on symbolism depicts a 'state of antiquity' from which unfolds various forms of human work, as a consequence of process of *sundering of sexual and working activities*. This has resulted into detachment of meanings of words uttered during performance of collective work, from their sexual origins. What he is depicting is nothing but socio historical origins of sexual alienation due to 'forced labour'! The formation of Oedipus complex acquired universal validity with sinking of the repression universally. . This reification , ossification of social acts over years, centuries, epochs has resulted into transformation of these 'words' through social repression into symbols. This has created their hierarchy and social institutionalization. This reification has fundamentally given birth to another type of dream distortion the Dream Symbols. *These symbols essentially defy Freudian technique of 'association'*. Hence Freud resorted to a 'supportive method'. In a way these symbols (as per Freud's Hypotheses) truly represent the thick bond between 'sexuality and human work'. Freud based his conclusions on transformation of solipsistic lives of human individuals, human hoards, and tribes into modern social order! The symbols are the result of repression ushered by enslavement of 'human labor', hence it is appropriate to call / identify them as 'desexualized - work symbols'.

The spread of commodity production and reproduction under capitalism has resulted into hierarchy of symbols, at the centre of which however lies the Oedipal symbol. The Oedipus symbol has the most privileged position in this hierarchy. The Symbol - Par Excellence. The identification and investigation into 'Oedipus Complex', the base station of solipsism, and bulwark of repression enabled Freud to offer a Science to the common man but the symbols resulting from *sublimation of sexual forces through 'labor' remained alien to his ' method of free association'. Perusal of this and working through the reciprocal relations between popular cultures and Dream Symbols* is done vigorously by E.P. Thompson in his 'The Making …'.

This passionately debated; Oedipus Symbol is the center stage of Freud's I.O.D. and self-analysis and as we have seen, is able to Comprehend 'two experiences' in Human life. Freud's founding of the method for pathological treatment of his patients is entirely governed by the Oedipal situation. It is the vehicle & life force of Interpretation and is the technique of handling resistances and experiences associated with it. The phrase "Working through "means overcoming the resistances, amidst the dynamics of conflict between repression and desires. These come into play during unfolding of the discourse, when the history is "Re" lived in the medium of Time, is 'verbalized', in opposition to /discourse of energy,

And also can be described as the strategy by which process of interpretation is subordinated to Self Analysis. By this process Ordinary consciousness tends to become scientific. As a inter subjective discourse Psychoanalyst also trains patient's 'ID' by attempting keep a step ahead of the analysand.

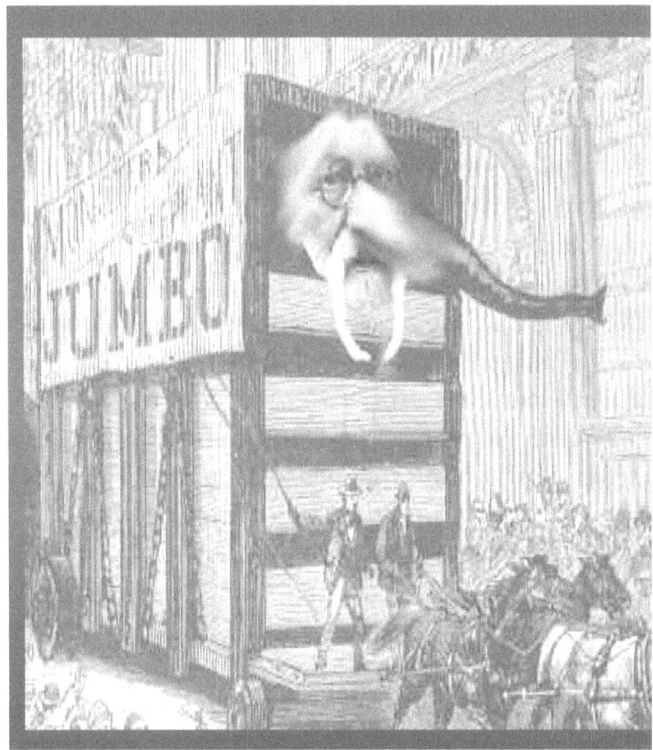

Patient's Dreams

Psychoanalysis claims to be the only Science at the disposal of Ordinary Consciousness armed with the method of Interpretation of Fetishistic Imagery and technique of handling Resistances during Discourse. Freud, who explored Oedipus Legend and its variant in "Hamlet", was able to discover historical transition from, symbolism peculiar to dreams and myths, to the ***Hysterical Symptoms and imaginative and creative expressions*** in literature, Works of Arts etc. The symbols detached from it's foundations in the field of literature or the symbols which I have termed as **desexualized work symbols**, or which are regarded by Freud as **another type of Distortion**, are born in the wake of advancing civilization. In short it supplements the Teleological and Progressive Vector in Interpretative technique in Psychoanalysis. By devising method of <u>grounding of the social alienation within Personal alienation</u> Freud offered historical explanation for ascendance of Dream Symbolism from its personal foundations into immensely wide range of human working activities and culture within the fabric social history.

In dreams and in madness, it is the cathexes from the 'nucleus of neurosis' i.e. from Oedipus complex, determines the regression or towards collapse into archaic. It is the work of self analysis and the technique of interpretation frees the future, present and history firmly arrested by primary repression and supplemented and overlaid by secondary repression.

With his theory of psychic repressions as internalization of repression through human social labor under the exigencies of Civilization, Freud has provided a way for enquiry into realms of psychology of the 'oppressed' masses. Contradictory role of Labor as 'exigency' and as 'sublimation' was not perused, by him further. It was left to E. P. Thompson to carry forward this task.

In I.O.D. Freud has addressed to various sets of tensions at the heart of Image, such as between, archeology and teleology, regression and development. Additionally important set of tensions / contradiction was due to sundering of sexuality and human work. The last set of tension worked on him since psychoneurosis implied break down of process of sublimation. His tryst with findings of Hans Sperber is the only attempt to relate sexuality to human conditions of work. By appropriating the findings of Sperber Freud was not only trying to assert the primacy of sexuality over human work, but was Grounding the Social alienation caused by new forms of sub sumption of labor in the inferno of Personal alienation (Inherited alienation), named castration Complex. Freud's conviction that "Castration Complex" builds the Foundations of Civilization becomes untenable, his method and technique of interpretation remains inapplicable to social history, and his theory of man and society remain 'a-historical' (as Schorske has identified) so long as *they cannot be firmly related to human work, on the shoulders of which this civil society has been created.*

(Hans Sperber)

This lack of articulated relationship between sexuality (erotic) and human work, exposes the glaring inadequacy of Psychoanalysis to embrace or even to relate to "strife " of Labor with Capital and transformation of 'Oedipus complex' by 'social control' and creation of Human wealth. This lack reminds me of famous critical remarks by Karl Marx on claims of Human Sciences.

"What is to be thought of a science which remains aloof from this enormous field of Human Work? Of a science which does not recognize its own inadequacy, so long as such a great wealth of Human activity means nothing to it. --"

Freud remarks in Introductory Lecture, "Among the instinctual forces which are put to this use are , the sexual impulses which play an important part; in this process they are sublimated – that is to say ,they are directed to others that are socially higher and no longer Sexual." (p.48) .The remarks definitely express Freud's deep insights into the nature of 'labour process' and 'capital accumulation. Freud was however more concerned with comprehending the modes of refusal of those sexual instincts to be put to that use. Their mighty strength and ability to shake the foundations of civilization he had realized in Social Neuroses and dreams.

One area which we have seen as remaining not – properly explored are his Auxiliary theories – specifically the question of Dream symbolism, which offers or <u>could have offered</u> a break through – revolves around symbolism in dreams, having reciprocal relationships with popular cultures of working masses may pave the way for integration with other human sciences. In E.P. Thompson's 'The making of ...' we may find the solution in sight.

From Dreams to Hysteria.

In the course of treatment of Frau Emmy Von N', a young lady suffering from chronic Hysteria, Freud came across reporting of number of fearful dreams of the patient under hypnosis.(In 'Studies on Hysteria').In the messages received during hypnotic treatment she used to outpoured number of several 'loosely connected stories'. After talking out of the stories she was again in normal frame of thinking. Freud found it difficult to reconcile this state of her mind with pictures she articulated during the treatment. Inner compulsion to articulate such anecdotes provoked Freud had already experienced strength of such compulsions in different field and in his own dreams. He took the trouble in writing down these dreams and solve them. He traced them back to two factors, firstly, ***cursory impressions of the previous day*** and secondly to *"**the compulsion to link*** together any ideas that may be present in the same state of consciousness"(Pages 124 to 127- Studies...).

Intense need he felt to undertake interpretation of his own dreams or to carry out some sort of 'self analysis' thus dates back to late nineties, that is much before he and Joseph Breuer published "studies on Hysteria". His insights into these compulsions are well pronounced in his remarks. "The senseless and contradictory character of dreams could be traced back to the ***<u>uncontrolled ascendancy</u>*** of this latter factor".

I have already dealt with; why at all Freud undertook analysis of his own dreams, rather than those of his neurotic patients. The reasons being that each dream would require long explanatory notes, preamble and historical records before undertaking interpretation secondly it involves presence of complexities in dream images hence from methodological point of view. This was obviously mandatory methodological prerequisite since he intended to investigate into "bewildering nature of dream work" It is clear that the discovery of dream work and it's constituents such as condensation, displacement, distortion and most importantly the Unconscious as a distinct primary system are products of Interpretation of Dreams .

Freud refrains from theoretically dealing with *identification of life force of dreams and hysteria till Chapter VII* where in he proceeds to visualize reciprocal actions of psychological scaffoldings constituted by two mutually interactive systems. Freud has already elucidated two fundamentally different types of psychical processes which are concerned in the formation of dreams. One of these produces perfectly rational dream thoughts, significantly as valid as normal thinking, while other treats the thoughts in a manner which is in the highest degree bewildering and irrational. Freud has identified the second process *as dream work proper.*

After a long journey through interpretation of dreams, in which he touches upon various aspects of Hysteria , undisguised expression of Hysterical phantasies during psychoanalytic treatment, **mechanisms of hysterical identifications** and hysteric symptoms, Freud articulates his first of the three important and distinguishing character features of the psychology of neurosis, namely, of hysteria.

Before doing so let me quote Freud who defines *Hysterical Identification in the context of how forces of individual sexuality assert themselves as a social force.* "Identification is a highly important motive in the mechanism of hysterical symptoms; by this means patients are enabled to express in their symptoms not merely their own experiences, but the experiences of quite a number of other persons; they can suffer, as it were, for a whole mass of people, and fill all the parts of a drama with their own personalities." (Distortions in Dreams- IOD P. 232).

Firstly the same kind of irrational processes, dominate the production of hysterical symptoms, like those in dreams. In hysteria patient also exhibits perfectly rational thoughts, in *its surface organization and as valid as conscious thoughts.* However, in the analysis of these symptoms, we discover that these thoughts have been *submitted to abnormal treatment.* "These thoughts have been transformed into symptoms by means of condensations and formation of compromises; by way of *superficial associations and in disregard of contradictions*, and also may be, along the path of regression. Thus there is a complete identity of dream work and the inner psychical activity which issues psychoneurotic symptoms. Here Freud is discussing the identity and difference between dreams and psychoneurotic symptoms and their compatibility with each other.

Freud restates this in terms of the theses he borrows from 'The Studies on Hysteria', which has already defined the hysterical symptoms as, "a normal train of thought is submitted to abnormal psychical treatment of the sort we have been describing if the unconscious wish (specifically sexual one), derived from infancy and in the state of repression *has been transferred on to it.*'

Second insight provided by Freud is again related to his imaginatively constructed psychical apparatus (resurrected on the basis of his Project of Scientific Psychology) consisting of primary and secondary systems' with whose concurrent action dreams are produced'. The secondary psychical process, which is the resultant of historical development of individuals and morality, is subjected to primary process and leads to formation of dreams and hysterical symptom. (p.767 IOID). The motive forces for both are provided by sexual and infantile forces which are invariably derived from unconscious. Thus he introduces the historical role of morality which works like a bulwark on primary processes.

The *Third* differentiation is far more vocal and explicit in its formulation. "However even though dreams and psychoneurotic symptoms both are the resultant of the same processes at work, *dream is not a pathological phenomena*. It does not presuppose disturbance of psychological equilibrium (of the psychical systems) and loss of efficiency.

Forth differentiation is that unlike Dream image, which remains solipsistic, Hysteria can be social expression of unconscious sexual desires through mechanisms of transference in which the present is treated like 'phantasized' past. Identification helps in 'hiding' or 'suppressing the past' 'Oedipal desires' by means of **Identification.** Freud states "Thus Identification is not a simple imitation but *assimilation* on the basis of a similar aetiological pretension; it expresses a resemblance and is derived from a common element which remains in the unconscious". (p. 233 IOD). For IOD through identification with singular persons--i.e., in terms of names, physical characteristics, gestures takes place by, transference of psychical intensities. Thus "it assumes the process by which emotions and desires originally associated with one person, such as a parent or sibling, are unconsciously shifted to another person".

These four differentiating insights founded on the *laws of formation of Hysteria*' as a complex Form arising out of *metamorphosis of 'dream work'*. It can enable us to make transition from the problem of formation of dream to more comprehensible problem of waking life- formation of Hysteria and Psychopathology. By way of analogy, we can say, from Marx's analysis of commodity and its forms of existence have identical relationship as dream and hysteria in which commodity and money still can exists side by side as forms of value. The essential life force in each case is provided by the **'dream work'.**

Freud's Methodology in analysis and treatment of Dream and Hysteria reveals a close parallel with Marx's analysis of Commodity and transition to its more complex Money form.

Making of the English Working Class

Application of Psychoanalysis to Interpretation of Class experiences.

Paul Ricoeur in Freud and Psychoanalysis outlines following criteria for developing proof of investigatory procedure.

A good psychoanalytical procedure of Interpretation should be in a position to 'decode the text of the unconscious'. It should be able to establish new coherence between all members of the series of 'psychic productions' namely cultural expressions.

The second condition the explanation is that it should be able to be incorporated and understood as 'work of analysand' and what 'happens 'to the analysand.

It should establish narrative intelligibility.

If all the three conditions are reinforcing each other they can be regarded as 'proof' of the investigatory procedure.

Freud did attempt to develop his own hypotheses of civil society, its discontent and its foundations. However one cannot say that he was close to offering anything like a social scientific theory even though he has shown great insights into cultural expressions or psychic productions on social scale.

Freud's concept of sublimation is only a shadow of concept of value and surplus value creation of political economy. Freud's schema can be represented as, instincts- forces of sexuality / symbols/ human efforts-work / symbols -works of Art or Created goods under the exigencies of life. Each bar represents repressive barrier on energy and human expression. Sublimation covers this three tier, three barrier process. Freud's interpretation of works of Art or created material and cultural goods proceeds with Imagery and enables Freud to reach into the realm of human experience.

Freud understood the crisis of civilization or as crisis of sublimation, as refusal of sexual impulses to obey the life exigencies and regressively return to their original incestuous aims. The (which

are always on alert). The frightening consequences of such process was experienced by him in rise of anti-Semitism in last decades of nineteenth century Germany and Austria, war Neurosis of second decade of twentieth century and it's aftermath the ascendance and
----
Conquest by Fascism. The failure of 'self regulated 'work disciplining' process under capitalism compels capitalism to ensure it's survival by banking on the most archaic, conservative, regressive and destructive forces within 'humans' (**after their fatal divestment from human work**)) which Freud had issued a warning to the humanity on the title page of the Dream Book, "*If I cannot bend the higher powers, I will stir up the hail*"

Freud was worried by the sexual holocaust and the social and personal dynamics underlying such a process. Unfortunately Freud had neither any mooring in Marx's theories nor had adequate understanding of dynamics of social history under capitalism. Hence he fail short of defining and comprehending it as 'work disciplining', process engineered by capital accumulation and fetishism inherent to it.

However his discoveries regarding technique of interpretation of imagery and theories of imagination in I.O.D., made deep impact and influenced the intellectuals, sociologists and historians of his times and the generation to follow.

The solipsistic, 'unintelligible', intangible', indemonstrable', mystical', fetishised' phenomena of the 'most obscure' regions Human mind, firmly rooted in the 'unconscious' now was de-fetish zed, exploded with Freud's I.O.D. and now became intelligible and tangible. Marxist historians and social psychologists have attempted to integrate these discoveries in their 'works' in their own ways.

In the light of inadequacies on part of psychoanalysis and Freud in particular to offer psychoanalytic applications to Human History I turned towards a discipline identified as 'psycho history' of which E.P. Thompson's works are regarded as part of.

This impact and influence of **Psychoanalysis** is explicitly discernible, in writings of Marxist Historian E. P. Thompson. Freud's fundamental interpretative discoveries which brought in the areas of Popular Cultures and Dream symbolism and underlying human experience within the reach of psychoanalysis have become the heritage of 'Psycho-Historians. His discoveries which enabled the 'archeologist' of the imagery to draw meanings through meanings and thus to reach out in to the realms of human experience certainly made an impact, on E. P. Thompson, though it may be though a devious route, through the influence of works of Erich Fromm, New left and Karl Mannheim's 'Ideology and Utopia'. His classical work, 'Making of ... ' has a clear influence of Eric Fromm, in which, he has been described to have offered' 'Psycho History of Methodism' a term closely resembling to ' Psychoanalysis'.

However every one from "psycho History discipline may not agree with E.P. Thompson's endeavor. Peter Gay launched devastating criticism of the Book by pointing out that, *"On the other hand, E. P. Thompson's Making of the English Working Class (1963) fails in this regard because the author's personal attitude toward Methodism resulted in an expression of his aggression rather than "an even-handed employment of psychoanalytic concepts and of historical methods."*

Peter Gay feels that "The worlds of psychoanalysis and of history are, and ought to remain, worlds apart. Still, the two worlds can enrich one another. Psychoanalysts can help historians deepen their understanding of motivation; historians can help psychoanalysts widen their appreciation of the social context in which persons interact" (Freud for Historians-By *Peter Gay* New York, Oxford University Press, 1985).

We take note of this criticism and begin.

"The Making ..." was originally intended as series of articles finally were published as voluminous and original work on History of the English working class. He has described the class as phenomena, cultural formation and as happening and not as a social structure. The central theme in a making of the working class, right from the period of it's subjugation (particularly under Wesleyan) to Methodism, to it's progressive self-realization in Chartist movement is focused on interpreting and comprehending experiences of the working classes'.

E.P. Thompson passed through a torrid and eventful life from 1940 to 1958, a span which included right from his role as a soldier fighting a war against imperialism to his role as active opponent of the Russian invasion of Hungary. British Communist Party's support to Russian invasion stirred him up from 'within'. Coming together of various splinter groups named 'The New Left' provided him the wings of imagination. But "The making" appears to have a deeper motive in the mind of this great historian, his 'revolt' against the Methodism his father represented.

Here we need to understand that this segment of the essay is *firstly*, to a certain extent amounts to transgression of subject of Investigation. Which is the culture the working men who lived through and created the in the process of making of History. The Imagery which E.P. Thompson interprets and deals with is 'Oedipal Symbol' social symbol par excel lance. It is a phenomena which is far more complex in nature, consisting of *images created during waking life* and individual and solipsistic imagery, including dream images dealt are as part of this subject, have the status of fleeting existence, undifferentiated from their social moorings. *Secondly* we will be looking out in this part for specific areas of applications of psychoanalysis, which Freud left unattended, namely E.P. Thompson's research skills in decoding the 'unconscious-Oedipal' text and establishing coherence in the psychical expressions in the making of the working class. *Thirdly* to recapture the 'lost experiences' which have suffered from '*condescension*' in the aftermath of 'Chartism'. Lastly E.P. Thompson is concerned more with 'waking life' of groups, individuals and classes, and not so much about the dream life and hence focus may be on 'Hysteria' rather than on 'dream life'.

In Freud we have however attempted to comprehend basic elements of relationship between Dream Image and Hysteria, the differences and the pivotal common ground for both, remains 'dream work'. Hence this common ground would enable us to approach 'Hysteria' more profoundly.

From IOD, Freud has stretched and implanted his discoveries in IOD regarding dreams, Dream Work and Hysteria *into realms of Civil Society* and where strife between sexuality and exegesis of life (labor) leads to danger of breakdown of civilization.

In EPT' 'Making... the path is exactly opposite of what we saw in IOD.

The Making---We begin with so called 'Civil Society'. For E.P. Thompson it was the most significant scientific work of History and milestone. It inspired him to take a complete break up from the tradition and allowed him to face the historically troubled situation. The surface organization of the Book is governed by its function as unfolding of socio cultural history of English Working classes, history of pre-capitalist groups, communities. To this he explicitly subordinated the social, cultural- psychical conflicts as expressed in the in dreams imagery and language, from one isolated period to other over eighty years.

In the process of investigation he reaches into the sub plot of realm of central conflict residing in the Oedipal situation of the classes and the exploitative mechanisms inbuilt in socio-psychic repression and into invisible personal narratives and the underground recesses of 'buried' self of classes.

Summery of the book in brief, runs like this.

The free born Englishmen under pre capitalist formations, surrendered their freedom and desires, to Methodism and other religious sects, which played out their historically assigned role of a theological, moral and above all ideological 'work disciplining' agency of the advancing capitalism. This was inevitable for establishment of Hegemony of Industrial Capital which lasted for seven Decades, beginning from 1760 to 1830. The Work disciplining role of Methodism acting as moral machinery was backed by legal machinery of the state and involved enactment of vicious laws like Corn Law and also had to surmount the resistance offered by Jacobian, Ludditsm and several other movements. Methodism succeeded in demolition of rebellious spirit of 'free Englishmen' by smashing 'Satan's Strongholds', by dissolution of 'Oedipus Complex'. This provided capitalism the foundations for subjugating large masses of working people and instilling 'exploitative mechanisms'.

What he did was to use his unique method of interpretation of imagery and talent in order to present to the readers and researchers experiences of ordinary men and women and rescuing them from "the enormous condescension of posterity."

The second part of the book offers exposition of how the 'reactive dialectic' inbuilt in theological tenets, of submissiveness (repressive work disciplining) and sanctification of labor" compelled the different segments of working people. The mass of working men and women affected by the misery, pain and exploitation ultimately organized themselves, several times, scattering and again compounding themselves for painful but exciting struggle against modern conceptions of property, and the rise of industrial capitalism in the form of Chartist Movement. The very image of 'crucifixion of Christ' became the moving force energizing the working people to struggle for their self discovery and self analysis for pursuance of truth and constitution of Chartist platform vigorously campaigning for self control. ***His 'The Making...'' stands out as brilliant picturesque, novel, unparallel and unique but exciting work of History***.

My aim is to discover his talent in presenting the 'psycho history 'of the working classes, i.e. application of psychoanalytic technique, method in this great work of History.

Interpretation of Imagery

It is interesting to see that in order to understand the making of the working classes and their traditions and the moral machinery which played the indispensable role, E.P. Thompson begins with John Nelson's 'Anxiety dream of Satan' reported in his Journal. Interpretation of Imagery seems to have been regarded by E. P. Thompson as the 'royal road' to grasp and know the subterranean workings of the 'unconscious and conscious' activities and processes. The first Chapter "Christian and Apollyon" more or less outlines his method in "The Making". By focusing on two mutually opposing important Historical trends, 'Methodism' on one hand and "Slumbering Radicalism" on the other hand – both preserved in the forms of variety of 'Imageries' at the level of community and traditions. Satan as I see it is the 'base station' of forces of sexuality is a very important Image in E.P. Thompson's interpretations.

E. P. Thompson has assigned central status to the role of Imagination implicit in both 'inner' and 'outer' processes within

Social trends and mass movements. Rather he has convincingly demonstrated that developing a method to grasp, *interpret and recover the 'lost experiences' of the men and women, and classes in the making is the task of the Historian and can best be understood and made intelligible to the readers through interpretation of Imageries projected or 'articulated' by working people and their representatives of those living processes.* A quote from the chapter 2 of the book will illuminate his approach.

"When we speak of 'imagery' we mean much more than figures of speech in which ulterior motives were 'clothed' (hidden but struggling for expression')". The imagery itself is evidence of powerful subjective motivations, fully as real as the objective, fully as effective, as we see repeatedly in the history of Puritanism. .... It is the sign of how men felt and hoped, loved and hated, and of how they preserved certain values in the very texture of their language. But because the luxuriating imagery points sometimes to goals that are clearly illusory, this does not mean that we can lightly conclude that it indicates a 'chronically impaired sense of reality'...... Whenever we encounter such a phenomena, we must try to distinguish between the <u>psychic energy</u> stored --and released – in language, however apocalyptic, and actual psychotic disorder." (p. 54 The Making ..).

**Young K. Marx and young E.P. Thompson
Manifesto to 'The Making of the English Working Class'**

**E.P. Thompson debates with Karl Marx on
Metaphor of Base and Superstructure Model**

- Karl Marx and E. P. Thompson

It is fascinating to read the book page by page to see how best he has integrated psychoanalytic techniques of interpretation of imagery within his own method of enquiry of a phenomena called , "The Making..."and which has remained within Marxist framework.

It covers working class History spanning over more than Hundred years passing through continuous alternating phases of rebellion and reestablishment of Authority of advancing Industrial capital marked with ugliest violence and immiserization of working population. Fundamentally it worked on annihilation of rebellious spirit of the mass of people. In this process role of Methodism as a rising ideology, as moral machinery of the state, and also provided sense of community to the working masses. In this dual role of Methodism as becoming the religion of the industrial bourgeoisie and spearheaded the *work disciplining* function

We see that work disciplining role could not have been played without targeting 'Satan' and it's stronghold. E.P. Thompson identifies Methodist Satan as, a disembodied force, located somewhere in the psyche, discovered through introspection as a phallic image opposed to the feminine imagery of Christ love in guts of mass hysteria which climaxed revivalist campaigns."

During sixties of eighteenth century Methodism made strident headways within the ranks of poor and working people. John Nelson drew congregations of clothing workers and minors to hear the new messages by interpreting his own Dreams of Satan, a phallic image, E.P. Thompson could identify John Nelson's 'Satan belongs to the world of fantasy' and the 'fantasy has the undertones of hysteria and of impaired or frustrated sexuality' (p. 43 The Making of---). EPT has a deep understanding of Methodism he founded in 1760s and relationships sexuality has with symbols, dreams, images and Hysteria.

EPT takes note of the Historians and sociologists of 1960's who have paid attention to 'millennarial' movements and fantasies and their significance who have discussed them in terms of maladjustment and 'paranoia'. Professor ' Cohn's remarks " It is as though units of paranoia hitherto diffused through the population suddenly coalesce to form a new unity ; a collective paranoic fanaticism".(p. 53 The Making...) E.P. Thompson questions and answers, " One doubts such a process of 'coalescence'. Given such a phenomenon, however, the historical problem remains – why should grievances, aspirations, or even psychotic disorders, coalesce' into influential movements only at a certain times and in particular forms" (p. 53 The Making)

E. P. Thompson has devoted major portion of his book to answer 'historicity' of the problem, why they coalesce?. . .

E.P. Thompson continues with his analysis to fix the historical milestone time of explosion of Hysteria as a Phenomena. Between this imagery (Kingdom Without and Kingdom Within) and the social experience there was a continual interchange -a dialogue between attitudes and reality which was sometimes fruitful, sometimes arid, sometimes masochistic in its submissiveness , but rarely 'paranoic'. The history of Methodism suggests that the morbid deformities of 'sublimation' are the most common aberrations of the poor in periods of social reactions of the poor in periods of social reaction; while paranoiac fantasies belong more to the period when revolutionary enthusiasms were released .It is in the immediate aftermath of French Revolution that the millen-marial current, so long underground, burst into open with unexpected force."(P.54 the Making --).

E.P. Thompson explores this in details in his Case History of Joanna and which is separately dealt with. He finds a royal road to interpret this complex phenomena of 'coalescence' through interpretation of dream like imagery!

Through historical references, narrations and quotes of poems, songs of clothiers, weavers, workmen, poetic creations and verses of representatives of the working people, E. P. Thompson has succeeded in reconstruction of the deeper relations, associative dependencies, between farmers and labourers, masters and weavers, Orators and masses, and **credible pictures and images of the times**, by way of excavating from 'beneath' the sociological categories and layers into the personal relations. In fact this recapitulation and rewriting of history by technique enabling us to understand his profound technique of interpretation and research into core of, what I will term as "associative Imagination" and the hierarchy of mediating symbolism is what differentiates E. P. Thompson from other Historians. E. P. Thompson has treated the specific images as having undergone condensations and crystallization similar to S. Freud's 'Nodal Points' in dreams.

'His methodology aims at rediscovering the **submerged condescended portions of** Movement of working classes which are trapped in pure documentation, sociological facts and statistics. It works thorough research work of the traditions, value-systems, mechanisms of economic exploitations of various groups, (artisans, weavers and communities) comprising the working classes which were subjugated to wage slavery The moral machinery, ideological ,cultural and social institutions rampage on their value systems inherited from pre-capitalist formations and living standards. Through chapter by chapter exposition, he enters into personal and individual lives of and personal dispositions of multitudes of people from their childhood, their living conditions, their communities, traditions and the process of economic and cultural process of immiserisation. This focus enabled E.P. Thompson to approach, grasp and comprehend what Dorothy Thompson called as 'History from Below'.

This is the region where he concentrates on grasping the inner psychical process, influence of Myths, operative and inculcated sexual -social symbols, phantasies, aphorisms and interprets popular sayings to re-articulate and understand the lucid imagery of process of subordination of entire mass of working people through psychic repression.

What E. P. Thompson is he defining is none other than the silent subterranean process of dissolution of the 'Oedipus Complex', amidst the brick by brick founding of process of 'collective exploitative mechanisms', This is what Freud favored to name it as 'process of civilization', to ensure surplus value creation to meet challenges in trading and mercantile. Both these processes fed on each other resulting into intensification of exploitation.

Presentation Methodology in 'Making of the English---'is novel to its core. His journey beginning with and through chapter titled 'Exploitation' passes through the experiences of various groups of working masses their traditions, role of political and cultural Repression, and their sufferings and enters into the essential and deepest collective and personal psychical processes of working people. ---

Here the focus is on interpretation of individual and group references of their Hysteria., their Dreams, day visions, madness, working of mythical mysticism, mass frenzy of cults during war years of 1801-4 which he calls as the Years of 'counter revolution'. As stated above, 'Hysteria' forms the groundwork of the book and E.P. Thompson is well aware of deeper relationship with dreams and dream work.

In this journey the chapter "Transforming Power of the Cross "stands out as unique and most innovative contribution in anything what 'psycho history' has created.

This chapter is at the center stage of the book. The chapter investigates into the impact of the moral machinery of state on to the deepest recesses of psychic life of the mass of working men and women and the work disciplining role of Methodist movement, Church, and Baptist revivalism during Industrial Revolution. Further, the Napoleonic wars were accompanied by more "Muted Forms of Hysteria "within working masses. Here Methodism was permeated with 'teaching of the sinfulness of the sexuality'. E.P. Thompson elaborates on 'layers upon layers of symbolism'. He exhibits deep insights into how the sexual imagery was consciously repressed and this (sexual and womb regressive imagery) itself was subordinated to sacrificial imagery of the blood. Since joy was associated with sin and guilt and pain with goodness and love, ' so every impulse became twisted into the reverse and it became natural to suppose that men or child found grace in 'god's eye when performing painful labor and self denying task'.

E.P. Thompson's insights into the intricate relationships between layers upon layers of symbolic-imagery, between sexual repression, Hysteria and intensification of collective labor only shows stand out as one of the finest discoveries

Transforming Power of the Cross–
From 'The Making of the English Working Class

Our sinner has now been 'translated from the power of Satan to the kingdom and image of God's dear Son'. And we may see here in its lurid figurative expression the psychic order in which the character-structure of the rebellious pre-industrial labourer or artisan was violently recast into that of the submissive industrial worker. Here, indeed, is Ure's 'transforming power'. It is a phenomenon, almost diabolic in its penetration into the very sources of human personality, directed towards the repression of emotional and spiritual energies. But 'repression' is a misleading word; these energies were not so much inhibited as displaced from expression in personal and social life, and confiscated for the service of the Church. The box-like, blackening chapels stood in the industrial districts like great traps for the human psyche. Within the Church itself there was a constant emotional drama of backsliders, confessions, forays against Satan, lost sheep; one suspects that the pious sisterhood, in particular, found in this one of the great 'consolations' of religion. For the more intellectual there was the spiritual drama of:

P. 404

Methodism is permeated with teaching as to the sinfulness of sexuality, and as to the extreme sinfulness of the sexual organs. These – and especially the male sexual organs (since it became increasingly the convention that women could not feel the 'lust of the flesh') – were the visible fleshly citadels of Satan, the source of perpetual temptation and of countless highly unmethodical and (unless for deliberate and Godly procreation) unproductive impulses.[2] But the obsessional Methodist concern with sexuality reveals itself in the perverted eroticism of Methodist imagery. We have already noted, in John Nelson's conversion, the identification of Satan with the phallus. God is usually a simple father image, vengeful, authoritarian and prohibitive, to whom Christ must intercede, the sacrificial Lamb 'still bleeding and imploring Grace/For every Soul of Man'. But the association of feminine – or, more frequently, ambivalent – sexual imagery with Christ is more perplexing and unpleasant.

P. 407

(– Transforming Power of the Cross)

'Two Transforming Experiences'
(Role of Crucifixion Symbol)

E. P. Thompson's magical definition of law of History, as perpetual or 'eternal condescension' truly reflects both, his insights into process of inevitable psychic regression and inversion and distorion taking place under the rule of 'Capital'. I have shown earlier a great resonance between Freud's discovery of laws of 'transvaluation' and E.P. Thompson's discovery of 'law of condescension in history. E. .P. Thompson's interests in photography and Montage provided him the technical skills to exercise interpretative technique on the imagery which has suffered from 'law of condescension'. From this 'condensed and condescended' past he has succeeded in freeing the history of common working people but also has succeeded in comprehending the two ends, regressive and Progressive discourses, in the historical process.

In this chapter are two discourses, one the 'discourse of the unconscious' and the other 'discourse of self expression'. The chapter has great resemblance to Freud's 'Typical Dreams', the 'universal experience' in typical dreams and 'the psychoanalytic experience'.

Two discourses are, two "deeply transforming experiences – one that of Methodism and the other that of political. Radicalism'. Weaving the enormous and multiplicity of experiences of the working masses and their leadership covering three historical time segments.

The *rise and consolidation of Methodism (1760 to 1830), ascendance of Luddism and Jacobinism (1790 to 1835), and Chartism (1810 to 1855), are three different processes with their reciprocal interactions stand out as extremely complex phenomena with innumerable tendencies and traditions flowing and shaping each of it dialectically, have been treated as if they are three layers of Images of a single Composite photograph. Like an archeologist he discovered the birth of Chartism within the ruins of older social order and the 'transforming power of the Christ'.* However the process of transforming the pre-capitalist labour into Industrial worker was completely subordinated to the rules and work discipline was something like a process of 'crucifixion'. ---

E.P. Thompson's a very detailed account and factual research in to this process was accompanied by his critique of Methodism and that of 'bourgeoisie's spokesmen' like Andrew Ure. E.P. Thompson's great insights into sublimation of sexual energies of the working mass of people are astonishing. 'His phrases like, 'it is difficult to not to see in Methodism in these years a ritualized form of 'psychic masturbation'. Energies and emotions which were dangerous to social order, or which were merely unproductive (In Dr.Ure's sense) were released in the harmless form of love feasts.... "(P. 405 The Making...). Or "These Sabbath orgasms of feeling made more possible the single –minded weekday direction of these energies to the consumption of productive labour'. (p. 406 The Making....)

E.P. Thompson's discovery of 'the translation of these processes into 'core of the 'First experience of crucifixion' is equivalent to what Freud Calls 'secondary repression' in which 'dissolution of Oedipus Complex is achieved. "The Methodists was taught not only to 'bear his crosses of poverty and humiliation'; the crucifixion was (as Dr Andrew Ure says) the very pattern of obidiance:'true followers of our bleeding lamb, now on thy daily cross we die… '. **Work was the cross from which the 'transformed' industrial worker hung**". (P. 406 The Making..) _"**Our sinner now has been 'translated from the power of Satan to the kingdom of God's dear son'**_. The imagery or phantasy of 'father son' Oedipal relation (in fact it has been demonstrated as complete imbibing of feminism and castration complex by working men and women) is now elevated to the higher level of fundamental collective work – capital relationship under 'civilization.'

This first **experience of crucifixion is** "the sacrifice which removes the guilt. …. It excites to obedience", (p. 402 The making..). This is the root cause of inversion, which is responsible for 'forgetting' and what E. P. Thompson terms as "Eternal process of condescension in history" which implants 'secondary' repression on 'primary'. ..

Methodism of 1770 to 1830 became the 'religion of the oppressed and by the oppressed' (Capitalists). At the psychological, level it was inculcation of repression, accompanied by birth, growth and rapid spread of Hysteria (particularly during war years) amongst the various groups of working masses in England. He has characterized the period from 1792 to 1830 as period of "counter Revolution" (p. 216 The Making). The historical span is marked by swelling the ranks of working people and growth of industrial capitalism; he shows in greater depths the Intensification of exploitation and enslavement of child labour. This was accompanied by misery, impoverishment and massive growth of ' psychical disorders' 'sweeping all segments' of Working class communities.

The second experience is of this intensified exploitation which is represented as Image of Crucifixion of Christ, which became the moving force of Chartist Revolution'. This dialectic within the well entrenched imagery of 'Crucifixion', in the wounded psyche of mass of working people worked itself out in course of History.

This condescension or coalasance of imagery of 'crucifixion' can be compared with the Image of 'Oedipus', on one hand as 'the castration complex' and other the symbol of '**pursuer** of truth'. In Freud's 'Revolutionary Dream' we see how Freud discovered coalesance of two transforming experiences in a single scene of encounter with Count Thun on the platform station. One going back to his infantile experience (you will come to nothing) and the current experience, of rebellion against count Thun. The intrinsic 'dialectic' of 'crucifixion has been well articulated in 'The Making ...'.

The rise and establishment of dominance of Methodism was preceded by anti authority agitations, mob risings, queasy - insurrectionary food riots and insurrectionary history of various sections of working populations in England during 1760 to 1820. Moral Machinery of state, Methodism and various sects worked as a repressive political and cultural force behind the state machinery to break the backbone of satanic strongholds. "Methodism particularly Wesleyans evoked the symbolism and imagery which are expressed in dreams and appear in psychic Disorders and stream of which is interpreted during psychoanalytic discourse.

Wesleyan teachings of sinfulness of sexuality and extreme sinfulness of sexual organs '(P.407 –Making of ----). Here author furnishes the details of the systematic campaign of Church and state machinery to revoke the *Castration Complex* in minds of the working people as precondition for ensuring sublimation of instinctual expressions as and through human *labor instilling the exploitative mechanisms*. This comes close to identifying the establishment of hierarchy and integration of two separate alienations. One the social alienation resulting from repressive advance of capitalism and it's grounding in personal alienation comprehended by psychoanalysis as "Oedipus or Castration Complex." Author continues "These – especially the Male sexual organs – were the visible fleshy citadels of Satan ---- the Identification of Satan with Phallus God is usually a simple Father Image, vengeful, authoritarian and prohibitive, to whom Christ must intercede ,---"(P.407 – Making --). The Father-Son dialectical relation has been worked out in number of forms in the Making.

We find innumerable illustrations in this brilliant work of E. P. Thompson to highlight how sexual and castration Imagery perpetuated and was "violently recasted the character structure of rebellious pre-industrial labourer and artisans into that of submissive industrial worker. " Ure's Transforming Power is a "phenomena, almost diabolical in it's penetration into every source of human personality, directed towards the repression of emotional and spiritual energies .... Displaced from expression in personal and in social life, and confiscated for the service of Church."(P.404 the Making ...)

Thompson points out that Max Webber has noted "the connection between sexual repression and work discipline." Most noteworthy process pointed out by E.P. Thompson is "But so drastic redirection of impulses could not be effected without a central disorganization of Human personality." (p.406 –Making ---)

The entire thrust is towards instilling psychic or ideological repressive mechanisms of sublimation of these sexual instincts of working people and resembles replication of Freud's "Redirection or Sublimation "of sexual instincts and their aims to socially higher aims"

Is evident in identical formulations. This 'disorganization', E. P. Thompson calls it as "pollution of the sources of spontaneity bound to reflect in every aspect of personality. ..., so **every Impulse became twisted into the reverse** (Note Freud's note on representation by reverse in chapter 'means of representation)... When performing painful, laborious or self-denying tasks. To labor and to sorrow was to find pleasure and masochism was 'love'. This strange imagery was perpetuated during the years of industrial revolution". (P.411 the Making...).

Further he says, "The utility of Methodism as a 'work-discipline' is evident. What is less easy to understand is why so many working people were willing to submit to this form of 'psychic exploitation'? How was it that Methodism could perform with such success this dual role as the religion of both the exploiters and the exploited? EPT gives three possible reasons. "direct indoctrination, the Methodist community sense and the psychic consequences of counter revolution". Out of this, the third reason according to him was the most interesting and important (the Napoleonic war years). In these worst years of industrial Revolution the 'hysterical aspects of Methodism and the Baptist revivalism played the most important role. Violent mass Hysteria and its muted forms were themselves the 'components of psychic process of counter revolution". **Even the 'indoctrination' and 'community sense' paved the way for symbolic expressions of sexual acts and actions. (Workful recreations of** 'chopping wood', 'digging' etc. as 'desexualized symbols')_were pointers to castration. Perpetual inculcation of Castration complex from childhood through Hymns and preaching in order to develop suitable exploitative mechanism of sublimation and for creation of Surplus value is evident in this Imagery. The mass Hysteria played the role of a psychical force to generate Surplus value through monotonous (drudgery) work in which hallucinatory fulfillment of sexual desire in this Imagery. The Hysteria associated with assault for intensification of Exploitation, accompanied by religious preaching on psychic life is further expounded by E. P. Thompson in these pages with highly rich collection and interpretation of Images.

"**Here we are faced with layer upon layer of conflicting symbolism**. Christ, the personification of love, to whom the great bulk of Wesleyan hymns are addressed, is by turn material, Oedipal, sexual and sado-masochistic "(P.407Making--).On subsequent pages Interpretations of Wesleyan and other Hymns is remarkable .Hidden and repressed sexual imagery underlying the extremely prominent womb Imageries are intended for his skillful grounding of 'work discipline' by strangling the rebellious instincts within psychic life. Such close grasp of psychical representations should convince us about E. P. Thompson's acquaintance and influence of technique of interpretation of 'Means of Representations' employed by instincts and desires.

I have dealt earlier with the Representation of **Logical Relations** and representations. (I.O.D. p.423 - 431). EPT's remarkable ability to deal with the imageries which have undergone the process of distortion and condensations, superimpositions confirms the influence of psychoanalytic technique on his methodology and treatment of imagery.

Imagery of crucifixion of Christ, the other transforming experience, has worked like an engine and transforming power_ in the psychic life of the mass of working people. The well entrenched imagery in the wounded psyche of mass of workingmen was simultaneously a liberating Force, particularly during the period of awakening of the Chartist movement. The *Patricidal, sporadic, individualistic "Anti-capitalist" impulse often exhibited in earlier 'mob violence' were translated and transformed into organized*

–semi organized trade union movements particularly after 1830.
The role of class leadership in succession has been grasped in the
context of their ability to accentuate the 'Catharsis', to play a role
in liberating Chartist Hymns clearly point out urge towards "self
–realization" by working men.

"Sons of Poverty assemble" refers to persecution of Jesus by "bad
men and wicked laws." Represented the Imagery of "Exploitative
Mechanisms" under capitalism and appeals them to "swell your
ranks, augment your numbers, spread the Charter far and wide"
(p.438-39 Making of ---). The imagery and Legend of Crucifixion
of Christ had transformed both, the submissive and the patricidal
impulses.' What is surprising is the ability of the imagery or legend
of Crucifixion of Christ to release the associative mechanisms
(catharsis) inherent in the psychic processes of masses like lightning
flash of hope and clear thrust for overcoming the dark despair. Out
of numerous techniques used by E.P. Thompson to get access to the
tension between the experiences under 'Methodism and political
radicalism' two important ones are,

1) Recourse to Imagery, to folklore, poetic and cultural
traditions within working communities during their
formative years and during important events of 'class
struggle'. The innumerable songs and poems referred, like
'General Ludd's Triumph (1811), cropper's song(p.611),
courage exhibited in Methodist Rhyme on the occasion of
execution before crowds(p.639),defiant verses of a prisoner
(P.773) point out to the ***progressive liberation from 'dread'
inculcated into collective psyche by regressive ideology***.
The Making... represents his attempt to **reconstruct their
heroism but not as patricidal vengeance, but as sharp
articulation of conflict between those who live 'by lust'
and those who live 'by labour'.**

2) Personality Model used to highlight the liberation
of Chartist leadership from 'hysteria' perpetuated by
Methodism. Formative years of revolutionaries from the
ranks of working men, like Benjamin Rushtom (1785),
William Ashton (1806), Richard Pilling and Innumerable
others, insights into their ***biography and personality mould***

conserving the childhood, their background as Methodist Preachers ran into conflict with their role as honest, dedicated activists from the ranks of working people in the course of agitations and trade union movement. Their persecution and imprisonments made turned them into Chartist heroes.

The interpretative technique enabled E. P. Thompson to comprehend "continuously generated tensions within the heart of religion "whose theological contradictory tenets" were those of submissiveness (work disciplining) and the sanctification of labor". Hysteresis represents "Return of the repressed while Chartism was progressive liberation of present and future from the clutches of the past. As EPT says, "Just as the repressive inhibitions upon sexuality carried the continual danger of provoking the opposite ..." Rather it was the inexorable 'reactive dialectic' inbuilt in theological tenets, of submissiveness (repressive work disciplining) and sanctification of labor" led to the

'Fullest development' in the latter history of trade unionism amongst miners, and rural workers and to the history of Chartism." (p. 437, Making ..)

If hysteria generated by advent of Methodism represents the compounding of the 'work disciplining' thrust of the capital accumulation elements of regression to archaic, on the other hand the ascendance of Chartism is something like 'self analysis' passing through moments of anxiety, through transferences and to emergence as a class, as a "cultural formations and having disposition to behave in class ways".

In what ways, the 'un perished', 'undestroyed' mental past (to use Freud's phrases) which was 'unabsorbed' by it's derivatives, was handled during these years? 'Self Discovery' and 'self definition' is the 'process of happening' in which "different groups of – artisans, workers and laborers – handle their experiences **in co-coordinated** way, come together to think, feel and act,"not in the **old modes of differences** and parochial seclusion, but in class ways." p.937- Making -----) This is since "class relations and consciousness are Cultural formations" .Self consciousness is posited and not given or available.

The role of 'Crucifixion symbol' in 'The making--- can be regarded as a close parallel to 'Oedipus Symbol' in the changed circumstances of History. If one is grounded in the dreaming life, the other belongs to waking life.

Tran valuations or Condescension in History.

'Army of redressers' is one such chapters which is dedicated to rescue "the poor stockinger, the Ludite cropper, the obsolete hand loom weaver, the 'utopian artisan' and even the deluded followers of Joanna Southcott', from the enormous condescension of posterity' (Preface p 13, The Making…)

The treatment of the subject and research techniques of this chapter brings to the forefront E.P. Thompson's outstanding interpretative skills and his eye for what is hidden and forgotten. In sub chapters, 'The Opaque Society' he elaborates the difficulties faced by historian in view of total trans-valuation (to use Freudian Term) suffered at the hands of posterity.

In selecting themes and furthering his enquiry he had to write 'against the weight of the prevailing orthodoxies, namely, Fabian Orthodoxy, the orthodoxy of the empirical economic historians and 'Pilgrim's Progress Orthodoxy', however he says, each orthodoxy has certain validity. The third orthodoxy is the major one, born amidst the social, political and psychic repression during 1798 and 1822 and subsequently in the aftermath of Chartism. "It reads history in the light of subsequent preoccupations, and not as in fact it occurred. *Only the successful (in the sense of those whose aspirations anticipated subsequent evolution) are remembered. The blind alleys, the lost causes, and the losers themselves are forgotten.* (p. 13 The making).

The interpretation of Luddite movement is a typical illustration of EPT's approach to historical investigation. In digging out 'Forgotten' role of Ludites, which has been isolated, banished and distorted, he says "historian faces difficulties in the interpretation of the sources which must be explained. From the 1790s until 1820 these sources are usually clouded by the partisanship". (p.529 The Making….).

It was very difficult for E.P. Thompson to traverse through the paths of plentiful information available on the subject, like archives and 'Home Office Records' to uncover the true shape of the experiences of the Ludite and the movement which ended on scaffolds in third decade of the century. E.P. Thompson comments, "From Dispard to Thistle-wood and *beyond there is a track of secret history, buried like the Great plain of Gwaelod beneath the sea.* We must reconstruct what we can". (p. 542 The Making...)

These resources are the secret and opaque tradition built by the activists and participants in the wake of merciless repressive laws 'against combinations'. The Ludites which survived or whose lives were spared after the scaffolds mixed up with new social and political movement, became the followers of Cobbett, Hunt and others. The reminiscences of these survivors and "it is indeed, the stories of survivors, began to break the surface of print in 1860s and 1870s and the local historians gathered them with sympathy and with some accuracy. Thompson says' "Because these works are the last forms of a secret verbal tradition, they must be taken as serious sources". These indistinct sources which have remained underground or unconscious so far "are the last form of secret verbal tradition, they must be taken as serious sources". (EPT- p. 541) These sources and manuscripts provided Thompson new avenues and energies for re-interpretation of History without discarding the value added by three orthodoxies of Historians. I will term this as interpretation of 'transvaluation or condescension' in History.

Case Study of Joanna Southcott.

Transforming power of the cross is also a superb analytical exposition of phenomena called mass hysteria, (I have compared it earlier with chapter Typical Dreams I IOD) to which large population of working people fell pray to.. EPT raises a crucial question, "Why working class people were exceptionally exposed to the penetration of Methodism during the years of Napoleonic wars" (and it's aftermath). As he investigates into it further he had to deal with Hysterical aspects of Methodist and Baptist revivalism.

During years, 1800 to 1830, the 'defeated and hopeless', working masses from various industrial districts, sometimes steadily and at times rapidly, embraced Methodism and various religious cults and sects, as a response to revivalist recruitments.

Like Ludites, E. P. Thompson has treated impartially the 'deluded followers' of Joanna Southcott. In his attempt to rescue them from the *condescension* they suffered from. In doing so, he had to deal with ascending hysteria of the time, both as hysterical phenomena and as a ' case study'. To look into origins and growth of Hysterical ascendance, he had to deal with the years 1798 to 1814 in detail, since this period is of remarkable interest to historian. The first frenzy of 'Joanna Southcott's cult made its significant mark during 1801 to 1804 and ended up with a climax in 1814, with her death. However the cult's clout, it's following and frenzy refused to die down till 1830, the year in which Chartism began to ride on political awareness.

This period 1898 to 1930, also coincides with consolidation of capitalist growth and that of textile industry in England and as mass hysteria clearly expressed worked as a repressive force against, the resistance of the political movements and drove it underground. E.P. Thompson has clearly noted that, this is the period in which 'working class turned to religion as **'consolation even though dreams inspired by Methodism were scarcely happy'**. As intrinsic to revival of Methodism and these cults, through out this period of industrial advancement, in manufacturing districts, "highly explicit, astounding as well as muted forms of hysteria" made strident growth.

What is interesting to the reader is how EPT explored the 'hysterical' aspects of revivalism and role of a famous case study? E.P. Thompson has vividly narrated the innumerable ways in which preachers and followers of Joanna, exhibited the hysterical symptoms, which at times resulted into violent mass hysteria, in terms of loud collective screaming, indecent expressions in prayers. In Karl Manheim, words, when the revolutionary spirit, 'ebbs and deserts these movements, there remains in the world a naked mass-frenzy and despiritualized furry". (P. 419 The Making…).

E.P. Thompson has identified this entire period as 'counter revolution', marked by 'defeats' and 'loss of hope' for mass of working people. To understand the pulsations of the years of hysterical frenzy, which sent tremors even in the Methodist camps, E. P. Thompson has banked heavily, for his research on books and number of writings published by Joanna Southcott during 1803 to 1805 and till 1809. To highlight the frenzy, and to understand origins of her own hysteria, he has given number of extracts from Joanna's, "Strange Effects of the Faith' and other literature and created a framework for a **case study on Hysteria**. If E.P. Thompson would have probed further into Joanna's dreams and her biography he would have developed it as detailed case study.

He narrates, how 'the emotional disequilibrium of the time manifested in the enthusiasm of 'Joanna' and the violence of feelings of the mobs, their apocalyptic fervor and hysterical longings for personal salvations. Joanna herself was 'the victim of her own imbalance and credulity.' Also she exhibited "pathos in her literal-minded transcriptions of her 'voices'" (p. 423 EPT). E.P. Thompson was tempted or rather forced to go into her auto-biographical details, to identify the **personal foundations** of her public, large scale, long lasting influence on the working masses. He says her appeal was curiously compounded of many elements. With vivid superstitious imagination of the **older England.** She herself was the Devon **farmer's daughter and domestic servant**.

Joanna was zealously attached to the Methodist 'communion' and could articulate the 'lurid imagery' and 'fervor' of the same. What is so fascinating in her communications was that the mystical 'doggerel' was amalgamated with her own style. Her literal minded autobiographical account of '**childhood memories, unhappy love affairs and encounters between** the stubborn peasant's daughter and disbelieving persons and gentry. The psychic regression and the 'renunciations of sexual desires' are brought under focus to highlight how these foundations of social hysteria were laid. The hysteria was also conditioned and fomented, above all by "war-weariness of these years..."

But why working masses fell pray to the Hysterical cult of Joanna, (E.P. Thompson asks) it can be explained by the 'identification' Joanna' could establish and create by fomenting and unleashing rhetoric focused on 'renunciation' of sexual desires (which came as her own hallucinations) and tirade and curse against 'landowners' and 'governors' who were identified as shepherds of England, and who 'conspired to raise the price of the bread'. In sexual terms they were identified as 'lovers and adulterers'

The mass of working people, whose plight' of the time was directly identified as the tribulations of the "children of Israel" and should renounce the temptations pursued by Satan. Joanna offered a shadowy 'Utopia' or 'Myth' of building up of New Jerusalem and return of the sacred land to the laboring masses and a promise to become joint-heirs with Jesus Christ. . Her followers were identified as 'Johannas' or 'Southcottians'.

The fury of the instincts was well articulated in Joanna's manner of communication which exhibited apocalyptic mood and a veiled threat of unleashing terror. "The earth shall be filled with "*My goodness*" *the Lord spoke through Joanna, 'and hell shall be filled with terror... my fury shall go forth...* " (p. 428 The Making..). Any one acquainted with Freud's Dream Book, will see its analogy with Juno's threat of 'shaking the foundations'.

Joanna's prophesies to tread the enemies in anger, "and trample them in my fury, for the day of vengeance is in my heart, and the year of my redeemed is come". These again allow expression to the furry of the instincts to wreck the civilization.

But what is so crucial in this case study is 'her appeal to the poor': in the sense that the revelation might fall upon a peasant daughter as easily upon a king. The extent and intensity of the appeal can be judged by the fact that her entourage included not only several educated men and women but former Jacobin and engraver like William Sharp, who declared his complete allegiance to her! Her appeal was felt most strongly among working population of the West and the North.

The Characteristics of Hysteria, as manifestation of superb integration of elements of 'day to day' happenings, (which are perfectly rational thoughts) *with the irrational, regressive childhood Oedipal desires has been well established by Studies on Hysteria.* On the other hand Interpretation of Dreams has focused on underlying processes and mechanisms identical to those of Dream work which result into 'Hysteria''. ---

Psychoanalyst will easily guess that, in the case study, the so called 'renunciation of wishes amounts to return of the same wishes under different forms'. In 1814 the cult reached a second climax "when aging Joanna had a hysterical pregnancy and promised to give birth to 'Shiloh' the Son of God, the hallmark of Hysterical Symptom'. The renounced desires are expressed through 'hysterical transference''.

This is the period in which number of sects of "new Jerusalemites' prospered in next fifteen years. This is cultural milieu and context of EPT's introducing the 'case history' of the greatest prophetees of all, Joanna Southcott, who came "into limelight with her cranky booklet, 'The strange effects of faith'.

Even after Joanna' died at the end of year 1814, the cult proved to be 'deep rooted. Number of claimants inherited her prophetic mantle. After so many rough tides it exhibited sudden flare ups and survived till end of the nineteenth century.

This remarkable case study or at least the frame work of the case study has been provided by E. P. Thompson as integral part of phenomena called Hysteria. More importantly he has placed *it as historically conditioned.*

Social Hieroglyphs in Class History
Resolution of Paradox
Archeology vs. Teleology

Dorothy Thompson (Professor of History at the University of Birmingham and E.P. Thomson's collaborator and wife) claims that this volume presents the greatest hits of the father of 'history from below' who marshaled grassroots data, and launched a scholar's crusade to reclaim workers –"the poor stockinger -- the Luddite cropper's memories – from the enormous condescension of posterity". *It is absolutely true that he "reclaimed" the same by devising a technique and method suitable to interpret the experience otherwise inaccessible so far to Marxism.*

By deducing from the strife between the capital and labor, the psychical forces 'by whose concurrent and mutually apposing actions class as a 'cultural phenomena' was made in the 'medium of time'. In doing so E. P. Thompson has enlarged the horizon Marxist vision of how the 'ordinary consciousness tend to become scientific, or how "science will be alive".

Making of English Working Class has demonstrated not only the relevance but essential nature of psychological technique of Interpretation, of rescuing their place in history who had suffered 'transvaluation', or 'condescension', succeeded in reconstruction of human history in general and Working Class history in particular on the basis of insights into psychical and social laws of history (the law of forgetting and representation of images). This shows the relevance of Freudian technique having a valued place in historical science. E. P., Thompson , son of a Methodist Preacher , his treatment of 'Methodism' manifests elements of 'Self Analysis' in Freud's IOD. In fact it can be stated that the lowest and the deepest desire of E.P. Thompson to carry out self-Analysis also is reflected as part of this Great historical Work.

The continuity and differences between Freud and E.P. Thompson can be summarized below.

1) E. P. Thompson was the first to integrate elements of Freudian theory of Imagination as of utmost importance and relevance for the History of the working class movement. Therefore, "Dream as psychical Phenomena" draws highly significant parallels with the phenomena of the class which was 'being made'. I.O.D. provides the readily available technique of Interpretation of imagery. Otherwise the same is unavailable in any other writings. In gist he has successfully integrated the much needed Theory

of Associative Imagination and Unconscious Imagination 'shorn off it's shortcomings'. Thus overcame the seemingly 'solipsistic' limitations imposed on Freudian theory. Best illustration can be found in Imageries of legend of Crucifixion of Christ and castration complex represent the progressive and regressive vectors of Human Imagination and mechanisms.

2) He was first to define the laws of history, closer to that of Freud, when he defines its Law as eternal condescension towards the past'. Freud's 'self analysis' and E. P. Thompson's 'self definition' or discovery' are identical concepts and processes. Both represent the dynamics of history and it's comprehension by technique of interpretation enable liberation of present from the past.

3) It is not to say that E.P. Thompson has exhausted the potentials of Freud's discoveries in Interpretation of Dreams. However he is the first Historian to lay foundations for a method of interpreting the imageries, like 'social hieroglyphs' result from 'eternal condescension and 'trans-valuation' and in "Reconstructing" the History of working Class. Most importantly his interpretation of 'Crucifixion Symbol' is equivalent to and as remarkable as that of 'Oedipus Symbol'.

4) Paradox discovered by S. Freud in treatment of "Oedipus Rex' and 'Hamlet', as is resolved in E.P. Thompson's treatment of Methodism and Chartism suggest that solution to hysteria and neurosis lies in 'preoccupation with social control'.

5) The discovery of laws of unconscious, namely, the law of condensation, Law of representation and law of transvaluation provided the deep insights into interrelationship between the technique of handling resistances and technique of interpretation of imagery. I have tried to deal with each of these laws (refer to the discussion above on 'overdetermination). Unfortunately Paul Ricouer fell short of exploring in depth the law of condensation and law of representation in his attempt to overstress

the law of overdetermination. With E.P. Thompson's contributions, application of techniques and methodology of Psychoanalysis to Hysteria, which had already become applicable for research of, –linguistic phenomena, creative writings, Art, literature, Cultural products can now be seen (with E.P. Thompson's contributions to psycho-history) as applicable to understanding of individual biographies, various regressive-reactionary mass movements and Human History. E.P. Thompson's Working out interpretative technique which works on both, 'unconscious' and 'collective conscious' is specifically the subject of this Essay.

6) E.P. Thompson took over the debate on Oedipal situation *from the realms of psychoanalysis and individual psyche into realms of History of making of classes.* Similarly his insights into hysteria as a social phenomena, its foundations in solipsistic dream work and underlying play of forces of sexuality is a great contribution to understanding of socially reactionary, retrogressive movements.

Psychoanalysis remains vulnerable and partially solipsistic until, it's marvelous and unique technique of Interpretation of "Word" and "Imagery" Its method of Archeological excavation to re construct history is not **integrated into revolutionary concerns of Marxism or interpretation of History**. E. P. Thompson's 'The Making ...' has brought Psychoanalysis into the Mainstream of History. By integrating and recasting numerous psychoanalytic concepts, subject of investigation (Human experience and imagination) Thompson has made history more perceptible and alive. The common ground between Psychoanalysis and History has been stressed by various thinkers. "Both history and psychoanalysis are sciences of memory ... and ...thus seem destined to collaborate in fraternal search for the truth about the past." But it was EPT alone did away with the Paradox between archeology and phenomenology.

Daniel Pick on the unwritten history of psychoanalysis in England says, "In a rare interview with the BBC, Freud noted how dearly he had paid for his "piece of good luck", namely his discoveries about the unconscious. Resistance to these findings, he observed, had been "strong and unrelenting", and "the struggle is not yet over".

In my view, as a psychoanalyst and a historian, the skills and insights of the historian are indispensable to the kind of inquiry into fluctuating cultural attitudes that we require before drawing conclusions about Freud's impact in Britain". (The id comes to Bloomsbury Saturday August 16, 2003- The Guardian). Also Freud's identification of 'Timelessness' and absence of 'logic of time' in their 'Unconscious' are precisely what Feud had to struggle with and discovered the 'historicity" in the making of a child into adult. Similarly E.P. Thompson well versed with Marxist Method and Techniques of investigation penetrated through the layers of memories (Layers of Imagery) down into the 'unconscious' in the making of the English Working class E.P. Thompson revolutionanized both Psychoanalysis and contemporary Marxism, and indirectly provided, a supportive, Historical method of investigation to Psychoanalysis.

In true sense, to reiterate what Peter Gay says, "Psychoanalysts can help historians deepen their understanding of motivation; historians can help psychoanalysts widen their appreciation of the social context in which persons interact". We can conclude that *Employment of Psychoanalytic concepts in true sense begins with E.P. Thompson's "The Making of the English Working Classes."*

I have attempted to summarize and grasp unique contributions made by Interpretation of Dreams the founding work in the areas of Imagination and Historical Research. At the same time I have not forgotten the warning from Karl Marx.

"What is to be thought of a science which remains aloof from this enormous field of Human Work? Of a science which does not recognize its own inadequacy, so long as such a great wealth of Human activity means nothing to it. --" . However Freud not far off from the truth in his understanding of 'Neurosis' as a mental product *at the root of which lies the 'sundering' of sexuality and human work, refusal of sexual instincts to follow the laws of civilization*. We are reminded of identical fundamental formulation by Karl Marx., when he says at the root of crisis of capitalism lies the 'sundering of use value of a commodity and its exchange value. The fundamental aspect ignored by the political economy!

What S. Freud calls as secondary repression can now also be understood as sedimentation and psychic internalization of process of capital accumulation and immense progress human collective labour achieved under the force of repression and which works like guiding channel for all human collective expressions right from Art to Social Revolution. It's breakdown or crisis, which S. Freud faced and could not comprehend during his latter years (Discontent under Civilization) merely demonstrates inadequacy of Human Science which falls short of addressing to Human collective work.

S. Freud knew it well that out of three contestants of Weltanschauung..., Science, Philosophy and religious, it is the last one, which is the most dangerous enemy of psychoanalysis, since it is has self contained, direct influence and enormous and strongest emotional power over mass of humanity. It fulfills three functions to fulfill, thirst for knowledge, it offers happy ending and comforts in unhappiness and thirdly it issues precepts and lays down prohibitions and restrictions. The convergence of these three aspects in 'god creator', the 'father' to a helpless child!

The scientific thought is comparatively 'still young' and still can counter religion only by 'establishment of progressive control over nature in general and human nature in specific'. Chartist Revolution which was obsessed with 'social control' showed the way and hope of countering this Religious Weltanschauung.

With E .P. Thompson's "Making of the English working Class " Marxism has taken a leap forward by internalizing the Methodological tenets and discoveries of Psychoanalysis. Now Class History can be grasped at Grass Root level and in better way and greater depths. By demonstrating that class history not only is governed by the laws of economy discovered by Karl Marx but is fully subjected to the psychic laws discovered by Psychoanalysis, since when both integrated and compounded helps to grasp the process of 'self discovery'. Marxism is more equipped today with its theoretical arsenals than it was before E.P. Thompson's "The making of the English Working Class". But has also exposed the glaring inadequacy of Psychoanalysis in its claims to be a genuine Human Science. And so long as Freudian discoveries and insights can develop into Philosophical arsenal of

Working Class in achieving social control. In the Prophetic words of Jean Hyppolite:

"It is only when ordinary consciousness recognizes itself in Philosophical consciousness and the latter in the former that, Psychoanalysis will be achieved, that science will be alive and ordinary Consciousness will be scientific."

Bibliography

- • S. Freud – Interpretation of Dreams
- • S. Freud - Introductory Lectures on Psychoanalysis
- • S. Freud – New Introductory Lectures.
- • S. Freud – On Meta psychology -The Theory of Psychoanalysis
- • S. Freud – Art and Literature
- • S. Freud – Psychology of Everyday Life
- • S. Freud – Civilization and its Discontents
- • S. Freud – Case Histories
- • S. Freud – Jokes and their relationship to the Unconscious
- • S. Freud – Project of Scientific Psychology
- • S. Freud – Historical and Expository Works on Psychoanalysis
- • Joseph Breuer and Sigmund Freud – Studies on Hysteria
- • Karl Marx – A Critical Analysis of Capitalist Production
- • Karl Marx – Selected Writings in Sociology and Social Philosophy
- • Karl Mannheim - Ideology and Utopia
- • E. P. Thompson – The Making of the English Working Class
- • E.P. Thompson – Making History
- • Carl E. Schorske -Fin-De-Siecle Vienna: Politics and Culture
- • Paul Ricouer – Freud and Philosophy – An Essay on Interpretation
- • Paul Ricoeur, The Rule of Metaphor: Multi-Disciplinary Studies in the Creation of Meaning .
- The Philosophy of Paul Ricouer – An Anthology of his Works.
- • Jack J. Spector – The Aesthetics of Freud – A study in Psychoanalysis and Art
- • Jacques Lacan – Speech and Language in Psychoanalysis
- .King Oedipus- Kenneth J Mcqueenie
- • Jacques Lacan – Four Concepts of Psychoanalysis.
- • S. M. Eisenstein – The Psychology of Composition

- • Essays – The structuralist Controversy – The language of Criticism and Science of Man - The John Hopkins University Press Baltimore & London
- • Sudhir Kakkar – The Scetic of Desire
- Sergi Eisenstein - (The Psychology of Composition)
- • John Mill - "The Unconscious Abyss"